As Above so Below

The tree of Life symbolizes a gift to humanity, a map of creation and a glyph for spirituality. It symbolizes Life with branches reaching towards the heavens and roots grounded to Mother Earth.

Healing in the Present Moment

By Linda Jenkins

Old Version
New Edition 2023
do not recirculate

5

Foreword

Things are not always as they seem for we are masters in the craft of illusion, and what we reveal of ourselves will never be perceived equally, as all human experience is judged according to knowledge attained. Sharing stories of one's life is not to create scandal, rather an expression of how insignificant challenges we face are compared to spiritual growth gained.

A purposeful recounting of early years to present day reveals a progression of emotional development and evolutionary side of being human. No secret of the ego is greater than what has occurred in mankind's history and concealing oneself only brings fear and isolation, a state of being that is felt as an absence of love. Life is like a woven cloth threaded by memories that portray the orchestrated illusion of our character in this lifetime.

As a practitioner of bioenergy therapy for 30 years I have witnessed emotional despair and physical breakdown from burdened individuals who repress "dark secrets" for fear of ridicule and judgment. Fears disturb our energy field and manifest into physical conditions over time.

Healing occurs through awareness of imbalances, focused intentions and reconnection with truths of our divine origin. We are magnificent energetic beings harbored in three dimensional forms.

Body fields are balanced when feeling peaceful, zestful and happy as harmonious creative forces in motion allow us to view problems as challenges for inner growth rather than obstacles of happiness.

I am clairsentient, but faith, and channeled intelligence has guided me through the labyrinth of life enabling me to have strength during times of desolation.

Look for goodness in the world and carry hope for mankind to live in gratitude and kindness towards one another.

PART ONE

RESUME OF LIFE

A cold and bleak January snow has fallen in soft layers for the last six days. The beauty of winter seems distant during the colder shorter days of plunging temperatures and howling winds. Snow drifts meander restlessly over crusted dunes while puffs of powdery snow floating in parched dry air glisten in teasing sunlight. I am a snowy hobbit peering out from my fortress of warmth taking comfort in the hum of the furnace churning out heat. The temperature high for today is -28C and the weather man is cheerfully announcing there is no wind chill factor hoping to replace desperation by gratitude.

Canadians are a hardy bunch that band together to endure the six month long winter disguised in balaclavas, toques, mukluks and layers of long underwear, sweaters and coats. Hidden somewhere in two months is spring and autumn, short seasons which are barely distinguished some years, but longingly anticipated.

We survive depression by planning flower beds from seed catalogs sent in February bringing hope that the longer, warmer days of summer will be glorious.

We drive on ice covered roads spattered with gravel for traction and plug in block heaters to keep car engines warm enough to restart as we race from one warm place to another.

By age four most children are skating or skiing, shielded from the elements by Michelin Man snowsuits with scarves wrapped around faces sporting ruby red cheeks and frosty eyelashes. Hockey is heartily claimed as the National sport supported by Moms and Dads faithfully delivering their sons to dawn and dusk practices.

Today the sky has a thick gray fullness which at any moment could burst open laying a fresh white blanket.

I think this color matches my mood anyway, the hue of gray, more of reflection tinted by a little sadness.

There are times thoughts wander back to memories of days gone by, mostly willing the happy ones forward but at times the other ones creep in from the cellar. An elderly man once said, go out in the world and take lots of photos and make lots of life because when you are old all you have are pictures and memories.

The warm tea feels good in my hands, good in my stomach, but it doesn't seem to reach my feet where the draft is determined to penetrate my bones.

I remember a visit with dad in Tennessee, sitting on the front porch swing in sweat soaked clothes reading for hours, absorbing the heat from a hot and humid August. My dad, inside the cool air conditioned house kept peering out the window anxiously checking if I had passed out from heat exhaustion. Hmmm ninety eight degrees and ninety per cent humidity… perfect.

Every so often dad would bring iced tea, sit and chat for a few minutes, then proclaim it was "too damn hot." I jokingly told him I had a lot of thawing to do after living through so many cold Canadian winters.

God… please don't let my heart take years to thaw…

Early morning in Tennessee is a pleasant time of day as the air is fresh, cool, and misty with dew and fragrant flowers. Birds and critters are busy replenishing themselves before they take refuge from the scorching sun and stifling humid heat.

I sat on the front porch one early morning sipping a steaming cup of coffee contemplating memories from weathered emotional storms and smiled remembering the times I had witnessed Dad doing the same thing after a restless night.

This was grandmother's porch where grandchildren performed plays, dances, and all other encouraged forms of entertainment; so much laughter. Grandma Minnie's house was a small white craftsman style structure.

The front porch was concrete flooring painted grey and a ceiling of blue painted wood.

11

Brick columns with black wrought iron arms touched the ceiling and red brick planters overflowing with prized flowers framed the front. Chairs of turquoise and salmon pink lined up neatly to watch the passersby of the day. The front yard had a large maple tree that provided wonderful shade; its trunk, painted white was surrounded by lush and neatly manicured grass bordered by pink peony flowers. Along the east side of the house grandma planted magenta colored Rose of Sharon bushes and a deep red Rose bush that was her favorite. It had been her mother's and when she sniffed its floral aroma it reminded her of her mama and childhood. Now under Dad's care, grandmother's garden was certainly suffering from years of neglect and lack of a gardener's love. The rows of overgrown iris now twisted and knotted were once sweet smelling beauties which I picked as a toddler and received stern reprimand.

Many of her prized rose bushes were now choked by weeds, but she would certainly smile if she could see her wisteria wound fifty feet up and around the oak tree.

Grandma Minnie always had delightful smells coming from the kitchen, her place of comfort. We were the lucky recipients of freshly baked treats and giggles from grandma's rotund figure, jiggling with joy.

My family lived on the outskirts of Knoxville in Sandbranch which is a community founded by great, great grandfather around 1830.

He wanted his children to grow up with religion and education so donated land for a church and small school. The valley stretched for miles with lush green rolling hills veined with prized marble and spring fed water.

As each child grew and married, they were given land to build homes for raising their families, eventually filling the valley as generations expanded.

One of these children grew up to become a fearless sheriff nicknamed "Shootin Sam." He gained his reputation from hiking back into secluded locations in the Smoky

Mountains shooting up "Still" operations producing Moonshine. His opponents were at a disadvantage as he knew every path through each valley, shrewdly rooting out well hidden moonshine operations.

Later, during times of prohibition one of the roads descending the mountaintops was nicknamed Thunder Road and "Lightnin Alley"as notorious ambush attempts by police lead to thundering engines firing power and speed to escape the chase and law.

To this day Sandbranch and Marbledale are still dry counties.

The house has seen a lot of life in its day; my father and his three siblings were born here and after Grandma Minnie died, dad settled in permanently, adopting his birthplace and raising his family.

When Grandma Minnie and Grandpa Fred were young they were notorious throughout the county for their tumultuous marriage. They could be heard up and down the valley cursing and yelling terrible threats and it was once said that every dish they owned had been thrown against each other. Their volatile tempers fuelled passionate love and fiery anger which created the pattern of their life.

After several years the arguing finally took its toll, and when my father was five years old papaw left his home, his wife and four children.

Minnie was left to fend for self and young family but was no stranger to surviving hard times taking comfort in the land that provided food and shelter.

Dad's younger years were tough to survive and with four mouths to feed during hard times, the children knew the meaning of going without enough food or warm clothing.

Dad used to tell stories of how they trapped squirrels and possum for meat and picked poke (wild greens) or dug tubers for food in the woods.

Minnie Magnolia worked as a waitress, cleaned houses and did ironing for the local community. The two oldest boys left school early to work in the marble quarry to help feed the family. My dad, at age twelve, hauled blocks of ice up and down the valley for long days and little money. When he was fifteen he travelled west to California with his cousins looking for work. They ended up in a pottery factory working for a poor wage, barely able to pay rent and soon realized the promised riches had vanished out west.

It wasn't long before the green hills of Tennessee called them home but finding no work when he returned Virgil decided to join the army in January 1945 and by June was sent to Germany during the occupation. He was seventeen at the time. Virgil was a corporal in the army and became a military policeman while stationed in Batoulz. He often spoke of the two and a half years in Germany with fond memories and stories he loved to re-count.

Dyma was born and raised in Denmark. As a child she used to gaze out over the sea and dream of travelling the world. She had three siblings and two caring parents who provided a loving stable home. Her mother noticed Dyma's keen mind and enrolled her in the finest school in Espjerg where she excelled brilliantly. Before she graduated eager employers offered enticing job propositions. Opportunity presented a little earlier than hoped for but excited to make a change she accepted a prominent position at Copenhagen City Hall. Social life exploded with dates and parties sparking a thirst for thrilling adventure. During the occupation of Denmark by Germany fate introduced her to a young officer named Verna who swept her off her feet. They were given just enough time to fall in love and make promises to wait for each other until the war was over. As he departed he placed a large bouquet of pink carnations in her arms and as his lips left hers gazed deeply into her eyes stating "I love you, wait for me, I will find you." After the war, Dyma waited with hopes of Verna's return but soon fears set in that he had been killed. A position was posted seeking young Danes for secretarial work at the U.S army base in Germany during the occupation. Her education and choices to learn English and German paid off giving her an advantage over other applicants. In her heart she felt it was her only chance to search for Verna. Listening to stories of care free days trading cigarette and chocolate rations for desired treasures, an intriguing exchange of currency, were always delivered with chuckles and a gleam of longing in her eyes.

Free meals, maid and laundry service and all the dancing one could ask for was a young girl's dream.

Dyma and Virgil met while he was guarding a border that she was passing through into Austria.

He teased her about the pink angora sweater she wore that emphasized her feminine shape and his flirtatious humor won her over for future dates.

Dyma took on the nickname "Bennie" because Virgil could not pronounce her name and Virgil became "Jimmie" for the same reason. Bennie taught Jimmie how to dance and soon they were winning competitions and each other's hearts.

They traveled throughout Germany and Austria falling deeper under the spell of love while touring the charming villages and countryside. For two years Germany was their playground, enjoying the blissful infatuation of youth and love. "Bennie and Jimmie" were married in Germany and as she stood with her lovely wedding bouquet of white calla lilies, the minister pulled her aside and gently told her that some of these soldiers came from homes whose families lived in mountain shacks. Although my mother's English was good, she did not have a discerning ear to realize my father's countrified background by the English he spoke. Besides he was very handsome and she was marrying for love.

Poor mother, I can't imagine how she felt when she arrived to her new family and home in Tennessee.

War bride and privileged to be married to an American was the community opinion. The only finery she had from her cultured life in Denmark was the paintings, and silver candelabra, acquired by trading rations of chocolate and cigarettes. The lovely wall lamps given as a wedding gift from her family, looked far too regal for the tar papered walls in their little home.

The young bride with her first child on the way had to haul buckets of water from a well across a field so they could cook, wash clothes, and bathe and that was just the way of life in the rural community at this time.

The pattern of neglect started early in their marriage. Each day after work Jimmie would eat his supper, bathe, then leave for the local hangout with the boys.

They didn't socialize as a couple very often, the days of dancing and parties enjoyed together in Germany were over and Bennie was lonely for her family. Life only got worse after her son was born.

Having no washing facilities the diapers in foul smelling buckets were a source of humiliation and embarrassment for Bennie. New ways of cooking continued to frustrate her as she longed for familiar foods and tastes of home. Her mother-in-law was initially hateful and full of mockery towards her mothering and homemaking but as time went on and people realized Bennie's strength and determination to make this her new home they began to soften. Minnie would slip bags of flour and sugar to her once in a while and others would give them extra coal to see them through the winter. Some gave canning and others friendship and finally respect.

Bennie tutored Jimmie to receive his high school diploma and finish courses at a business college.

They moved to Nashville looking for a fresh start where they bought a new house and newer car. There were no furnishings except for the bedrooms, kitchen and the beautiful wall lamps which hung on the empty living room wall.

Brother Danny was a precocious and bright child. Once when Minnie visited, she apparently asked Danny to do something he didn't like so he took the water hose and at full blast sprayed her through the screen window soaking her and the new hardwood floors. Instead of being angry she just stood there laughing and jiggling until she wet her pants.

I think one adjustment mother could never make was to laugh at self and surroundings.

She was introduced to a culture where people worked hard to present life as easy going, worry free, and full of trivial humor. Laughter was sacred and established many years before as the medicine to get through the misery.

In July 1952 I was born on Grandma Minnie's birthday into a life of complete chaos; my arrival into the world could not have been at a worse time. Coming home from the hospital colicky meant mother cooked meals with me hanging on her hip or shoulder while looking after a busy son, home and husband. There was no domestic help from Jimmie and the move to Nashville had been to separate him from the boys club, a new start, but it wasn't very long before he returned to his old ways of seeking entertainment.

Bennie was suspicious of Jimmie having an affair because he would call out the name of another woman in his sleep.

One day Bennie took a pencil and traced over a number Jimmie had scribbled, called, and hearing a woman's voice had the dreaded suspicion confirmed.

She confessed to her neighbor Mrs. Morgan what was going on and the two conspired to follow him. When he backed out of the driveway Bennie grabbed her infant laying her in the back seat and the two women nervously tailed the black Chevy.

On one hand Bennie was hurt and angry, on the other she was afraid to confront the truth having an infant, a four year old, no family and no job or money to live on.

They pulled up in front of a restaurant popular with locals, carefully parking out of sight. It was a casual eatery with a jukebox playing tunes that brought back memories of war, reminding everyone how great peace time was.

Small tables of grey marbled arborite and red vinyl stools brought life into the smoky atmosphere.

Jimmie walked in to meet Judy, a pink scarf tied through her blonde hair, sipping on a coke through a red lipstick coated straw. Jimmie slipped into the booth sliding his arm around Judy and had barely said hello when Bennie burst into the room with her infant in arms, glaring through the smoke filled room focusing on her target. Enraged yet deadly calm she walked over, shoved her infant into Jimmie's arms, turned her attention to Judy and venomously said "you have something that belongs to me and I want it back."

The beautiful tri-colored gold wedding band that Bennie had purchased in Germany for Jimmie was on Judy's hand. Bennie's eyes were like blades of steel ready to slice open her victim and Judy lamely said she did not know Jimmie was married with children. Their voices grew louder, yelling over the screaming infant and people were looking, listening, and whispering about the unfolding human drama.

Judy indignantly huffed, slammed the ring down on the table and stomped out.

Bennie got her ring back only to throw it into the muddy Tennessee River never wanting to see it on anyone's hand again. Jimmie apologized, promising it was over and pleaded for forgiveness while the infant in the back seat distressed from hours of no food or attention, wailed her displeasure as they drove back home.

I cannot imagine the emotional pain mother endured at this time in her life, an ocean separating her from family, no money, two small children and an unfaithful husband.

I hope she dreamed of times she pick-nicked along the Rhine River with other beaus, or bicycled with her girlfriends throughout Denmark's lovely countryside and beaches.

I hope she relived her carefree days in the army flirting and dancing with young men as all young women did.

I hope she dreamed of cozy nights in her childhood home listening to stories on the radio, comforted and secure, while the family shared tea and pastries.

I hope she remembered the boisterous laughter of uncles and aunts visiting on Christmas Eve as they sang and danced around the tree. Festive decorations, china and crystal gleaming in candle light from silver candelabras, set upon finely stitched table linen, awaiting a feast of succulent roast, and baked goodies for the occasion. Fine paintings and furniture filled rooms from money her mother and father had scrimped and saved for buying their dreams.

I hope she dreamed of New Year's Eve galas where feasting and gaiety and fancy dresses of silk swished in ballroom waltzes until a New Year dawned. We need our dreams in such times of harsh and cruel reality.

After being caught and feeling guilty from his affair it was decided to temporarily separate and send Bennie to her family. Since Denmark was out of the question, the only choice for Jimmie was to drive his wife and two children to Canada where Bennies brother had recently immigrated. After a long grueling week of driving three thousand miles, we arrived with all our belongings packed for an undetermined length of stay. My uncle's family lived in a small house, certainly no room for guests and struggling financially themselves, yet here we stood on their door step, left at the mercy of Mom's brother for our survival.

It was our first taste of Canadian winter and we were totally unprepared with flimsy clothing to protect us from the frigid temperatures.

Wooden crates became our table and chairs and thin blankets did little to ease our discomfort from the drafts of winter.

Mother took a picture of us standing in a snowdrift in the "bald ass prairie;" not a tree or bush in sight.

Jimmie had taken a job in Ohio for a better wage in order to save money to relocate us to Denmark. Dad agreed that moving to Europe was a good opportunity as there were no jobs in Tennessee and looked forward to a better life.

My grandparents had an apartment ready and waiting for us in Denmark, excited that we were coming.

Three months later a letter arrived with train tickets from Jimmie for Bennie to come back to Tennessee. Bennie said she wanted to come home to Knoxville instead of going directly to Denmark and dad was happy with the decision since he missed his wife and family.

We moved back to Knoxville across the French Broad River to the community of Sandbranch. Each Sunday we went to the Baptist church built on great, great, grandpas donated land singing and fanning ourselves through the heat of the sermon and summer. After many Amens and handshakes we joined the parade of people dressed in their Sunday best adorned with hats and gloves to walk down Thorngrove Pike waving salutations at neighbors who had already managed to find their seats in the cool breeze of their front porches.

It would be a lunch of fried chicken, mashed potatoes with chicken gravy, green beans, fried okra, corn bread, pinto beans, and chess pie or chocolate cake, with iced tea to drink. Yes, grandma's kitchen was a place of comfort that we gratefully shared.

It was on those afternoons we sang and danced on the front porch while our parents leaned back heavily in their rockers. When hats began tipping low over foreheads, we knew it was our cue to disappear into the woods for an afternoon of exploration and games.

The pungent odor of earth's decay and renewal from the mossy floor of the forest still remains a strong trigger to childhood memory.

Our gatherings of wild herbs taught to us by Grandma Minnie enriched life with knowledge of nature's medicines. There is primal pleasure in digging sassafras root bold in licorice flavor for a good chew or cup of tea. Our medicine chest was the forest for treating colds, and common childhood ailments.

Bennie and Jimmie sold their possessions and gave their farewells to family in Knoxville. The decision was made that we would travel ahead of dad to set up our home.

Mom, Danny and I traveled by train to New York, boarded a ship for crossing the Atlantic to Rotterdam, and completed our journey by train to Espjerg, Denmark. Memories of mother during our visit are happy and laughing with family, excited to show us her childhood home and relatives even if we couldn't speak the language.

The trip would not have been complete without visiting Tivoli Garden in Copenhagen; naturally a child would remember riding a man-made white swan in a lagoon surrounded by beautifully lit gardens and fantasy characters wandering the park.

Danny and I were perfectly content with celebrity attention from family. Neighborhood girls delighted in pushing me on the swing giggling with surprise at the mysterious crinoline from American fashion.

During our three month stay father continued to write his passionate love letters pulling at mother's heart. Bennie encountered difficulties with her mother as personality differences surfaced during their visit leaving her to conclude that moving back home to Denmark would be intolerable. It was during this visit my grandmother revealed a devastating truth to mother. Grandmother had received a letter from Verna while Dyma was in Germany but destroyed it because Dyma was already engaged to be married. Verna had been taken as a prisoner of war for two years and had no way of contacting anyone until his release. Hearing this news Dyma was emotionally shattered, feeling angry and betrayed by her mother. Two crossroads had steered her future and destiny. Firstly, if her mother had given Dyma the letter before marriage would Dyma have ended up with her first love? I believe the answer would have been yes. She moved on after two years of waiting fearing him to be dead. I found a letter written by Mom at age seventy to Verna explaining how the letter was destroyed, never discovering the truth until years later but of course it was never sent because she could not locate him. It remained a painful regret and unfulfilled wish to reconnect with him for the rest of her life. From many conversations about him over the years I knew she continued to remember him as her lost love. Secondly, bitter resentment towards her mother fuelled her decision without consulting Jimmie to return to Tennessee just as father was to depart.

Jimmie was devastated to see their well made plans falling apart after working and saving for a year. He felt downtrodden and hopeless.

Tearful farewells, a last time of seeing grandfather and another crossing of the Atlantic brought us back to the gates of hell.

Mother's diamond ring had been stolen and more secrets began surfacing. Dad met a girl who was seventeen years old at the swimming pool while we were in Denmark and during the following year our parents were constantly fighting from the betrayal and unraveled future plans.

The final drama took place in our parents' bedroom as Dan and I witnessed with terror filled eyes angry parents screaming profanities, and Dad declaring Mom crazy, flung her across the room. At that point all four of us became crazy in the family drama.

As children our world was in upheaval from parents absorbed in their misery from poor choices. It was a time of horror and physical retching from fear.

Father began packing his suitcase to leave us for good and Danny disappeared. I grabbed onto father's ankles crying and begging him not to go away. Mother was hysterical. Out on the street as he threw his belongings into the trunk of his black Chevy with the whole world to hear wailed a mother and daughter for the man in their life not to leave.

In the following months mother attempted an appeal to the girl's family taking us to their home, hopeful that a guilty conscience from leaving children fatherless would have effect. There was nothing there except humiliation.

While Danny and I watched, our father sat in the rocker with his girlfriend on his lap. Her family sat jeering and laughing at the three of us standing in the doorway.

The seventeen year old girl was pregnant, dad was threatened by her family to do the right thing, and his balls were finally in a vice. My parents were divorced as I turned six.

Officially we were ostracized from Sandbranch and Sundays on grandma's front porch. Danny and I did our best to adjust but retaining the innocence of childhood through the cloud of loss, pity and being forgotten took its toll.

Mother leaned heavily on her son for advice who took it upon himself to be the man of the house. I slid into the pretend world of paper dolls and sought solace in the woods as awareness of poverty set in. Treats came occasionally in the form of banana splits we made if any money could be spared. Mother made our home cozy and warm with her magic touch of decorating with little funds. She sewed most of our clothes and it was understood that we never ask for anything.

I remember once asking for money for school supplies, and in a flash my brother glared sternly informing me that mom didn't have money for extras.

At Christmas there always seemed enough for extras, treats and presents and the only time of year dad could visit without animosity.

It was nice to be together and dream for the evening that life was normal. I remember one Christmas Eve, during the usual whining and wishing for a white Christmas, looking out to see silver flakes of snow reflected by streetlight softly drifting down upon the trees. We stood on the front porch witnessing a magical moment as snowflakes the size of silver dollars fell silently, softly down in a warm calm winter's night.

Tree branches heavily laden with glistening flakes filled our world full of a million twinkling silver stars.

We just stood there in awed silence hugging each other while nature gave a magnificent gift.

I always enjoyed when dad took me shopping for a new school outfit, or winter coat pausing for lunch in a fancy restaurant downtown. Dad worried about whether we were warm, always making sure we had proper winter clothing.

It also meant a visit to his place of work where paraded through every department his fellow employees could measure how much I had grown. I remember being amazed that dad seemed to know everyone in Knoxville striking up cordial conversation wherever we went. He had a charismatic personality that drew people like bees to honey and lingering laughter from his latest joke trailed behind him.

Dad came to the house for visits, sometimes taking us to the Zoo or Kay's Ice Cream Parlor, but slowly we drifted farther apart into separate lives. He had a new wife and baby girl to look after and eventually I accepted our lives had changed forever. I liked his wife and my half-sister, Dan however felt a protective allegiance to mother and since they were responsible for her pain, rationalized not to accept them into our lives. It was all very confusing trying to keep secrets from visiting grandma's house where the new wife and baby lived and I was troubled within whether I was betraying mother by wanting to spend time with father. Emotionally I knew mother was fragile and insecure needing attention and support which Dan and I tried to provide as we were all she had.

It was during this time that people would comment on how shy I was, and true enough I was a quiet child. I remember as a child being introversive, intensely observing everyone and everything around me realizing early on that I was pretty much on my own. I felt no resentment, but through emotional chaos I learned emotional independence.

As a child I understood the adults around me were self-absorbed, and feeling invisible to them detached and became comfortable within myself.

Throughout life going within for answers reliably gave me truth and counsel I needed. Somehow I instinctively knew this was how to access information for solving my problems.

Although my first memory of what I call "knowing things" occurred at age four the actual feeling of another presence was not until age six. I became aware of a trusting intelligence and guidance from an invisible source; some would call this a guardian angel.

Mother took us to a photographer and as we stood close together I "felt stories" about him. I looked up at mother and said "Mommy his heart is sick" to which both people startled because he indeed had a severe heart condition.

A few more incidents occurred and finally mother, so disturbed, forbade me to ever speak about people like that again. I was hurt, confused and sad that I had fallen out of favor; I felt I had been bad. The reprimand enhanced my shyness, and during further encounters I stood with eyes squeezed tightly shut trying to block out any information.

As I grew older, in secret, I continued using high sense perception to my advantage especially during school years with teachers. It also gave me sensitivity towards friends providing an understanding to their situations with few words needed. It made me aware of bad thinking people and dangerous situations to avoid.

My first exposure to alcohol came from Grandma Minnie's second husband Mr. Waldrop. I remember hearing stories and whispers about him and knew there was something people did not approve of, but he was always friendly and kind. I studied him a little closer listening to conversations with intense interest or asking him direct questions, trying to figure out the problem.

When I was seven years old Mr. Waldrop got up early one beautiful summer morning while the dew and mist were still heavily rising from the French Broad River.

The river was swollen and muddy from spring rains, lazily winding its way through the weeping willows along its banks. Someone seemed to recall seeing a man walk onto the bridge but the sun was just rising and most were still in bed. Poor Mr. Waldrop jumped into the muddy water that early morning, ending the misery that was too much for him to bear. I walked up to his open casket, my first experience of death, and peered into his face noticing bruises, wondering if it had hurt as he hit the water.

Later I heard the whispers about alcohol, cancer, money, Minnie, and poor man. I was irritated at their previous mockery; now they were sad and missing their friend.

Death seemed to stay on my mind for a long time. Each time an animal died I built elaborate caskets and performed ceremonial burial services. No one could answer my questions about death, and feeling deeply troubled, pondered about who would die next.

My mind lingered in perplexity and mystery ever watchful and curious.

As mother sorted out life after divorce she juggled the demands as head of household with confidence but her roles of bread winner and mother were stretched thin with the pressures of time. I became very quiet knowing it made life easier, overhearing Mom say it was a relief that I played quietly for hours with my dolls.

By chance, I went to church with one of our neighbors and while in Sunday school an amazing joyful door opened as our teacher told a story of Jesus. It was like awakening from a dream, lost yet familiar, as I happily declared to anyone who would listen that I had a new best friend.

Each day I spoke to Jesus about everything, feeling love in my heart that filled me with happiness and laughter.

My parents, neighbors and friends heard me having lengthy conversations to which their curiosity forced them to ask to whom was I speaking. I can assure you no one ever had the nerve to suggest it was a make believe friend.

I rode my bicycle in the middle of the day to church, walked right up to the statue of Jesus and continued to talk for as long as I wanted and no one ever came in to interrupt me. I wonder to this day did no one look after the church leaving the door wide open or was someone in the background just listening to this wayward child? I climbed the highest trees in the woods and sat at the top having grand conversations with Jesus, feeling protected and perceiving danger in life with uncanny intuition. My life changed drastically, I was no longer a shy withdrawn little girl.

It was a memorable day when Luella arrived, finally, another girl to bring balance in an all boy neighborhood. Imagination, laughter and play took over our days in carefree abandon as good fortune gave us four very happy years together on Michael Street. Living only two houses away from each other Luella and I were kindred souls with uninhibited imaginations that could hardly wait for each day to begin our adventures in the woods. We built a secret fortress from willow branches along the creek where we enjoyed sandwiches, secrets and stories. Handmade fishing poles with a chicken bone dangling on the end captured many cranky crawdads. There was no thrill greater than being chased in the cornfield by an angry ten foot long black racer snake. Screams heard throughout the neighborhood only attracted other kids who wanted to feel the thrill of adrenaline racing through their heart from fear.

There have always been bullies who make your eyes blink and breath quicken at the mere sight or rumble of their voice and Gary Smitty was no exception. He would pinch or hit anyone that got in his way, bellowing bullish laughter as he abandoned his recoiled victim. Retaliation only fuelled further torment assuring your yard would be the next target of toilet paper strewn throughout trees waving reminders he was watching you. Hours were spent high up in trees in seething humiliation clearing the mess while snickers from behind the hedge created buckets of self-pity, for no friend would dare to be seen helping. Many a battle took place with good guys and bad guys lining up on opposite sides of the creek.

Slings made of cloth were stuffed with rotten apples for ammunition as each opponent desperately clung onto thirty foot long strands of weeping willow branches that propelled us back and forth across the creek to unload on our target. The mushy splats made a hollow sound as they connected and soon a slippery ground saw a mass of bodies hopelessly trying to gain foothold for remaining upright. Eventually someone would gratefully call a truce and sticky gooey bodies were met by disgusted Mothers who insisted the only way back into the house was to be hosed down outside.

My sensitive radar picked up "feelings" about Luella's father sensing he had problems, but due to past reactions from mother I was cautious to speak of it. One evening I asked a question to which Luella's mother overheard and responded by saying Luella's father worked very hard and had to take medicine when he came home to relax.

The medicine was alcohol. I inadvertently discovered the liquor while playing in Luella's house and knowing this was how Waldrop died became alarmed for my friend as I pondered over what could prevent a tragic ending. I began observing her father more closely and chatting with him more often finding him to be a soft hearted, sensitive soul caring deeply for his family but tormented by his weakness to overcome his inner demon.

There were nights I joined Luella and her Mom for a trip to the Library or movie theatre when her father was having a difficult time. His drinking took its toll on their family and eventually he moved away for a "long visit" with relatives. Luella never spoke of her dad's drinking and how it affected her life.

Maybe that code of ethics is a southern thing, not speaking of "uncomfortable" topics, locking secrets away. I had observed that far off look several times in my dad and grandma when I broached family inquiries, a silent communication which meant that unpleasantness is an unspeakable topic.

I am sure God chose the South when he thought of spring, as there can be no other place that nature unfolds with such magnificent beauty. Every tree, bush and flower begins to bloom in pretty little dresses painting a landscape with a multitude of colors. It seems as close as it gets to the Garden of Eden. In the changing seasons of Mother Nature I found solace, witnessing God's blessings and promises each day I awakened in my beloved South.

I knew God's presence was strong in the forest and it became my church for prayer as a small child.

So it was that Dan and I grew up on Michael Street in Knoxville Tennessee. We were free to develop our spirits with neighborhood friends throughout carefree days, healed from divorce by the hands of nature and time.

Somehow Mom managed to weave a very close family web around us bound with love and devotion that cocooned us from harsh reality.

Our family outings were simple; the annual Fair at Chilhowie Park, a swim at Alcoa pool, and occasional visits to the Zoo and miniature golf kept us content.

Our simple lives were soon to come to an end.

O Canada

One day family from Canada suggested we move north to live close to them as Mom was now on her own. Moms loneliness and wish to be with her brothers and sister had been discussed several times.

Dan and I waited for the uncle we had never met to arrive from the cold country in the north. He got off the plane in July wearing a wool suit sweating and gasping for air. He spoke with a very strange accent and our impression was that he was quite peculiar.

The packing and sorting of our possessions began in earnest filling a U-Haul trailer pulled by a green tank of a car, a 1938 Oldsmobile. I had no idea at the time my life would be changed forever. As we drove down the tree lined street surrounded by things familiar and loved, I saw through tears my father standing in the middle of the same road he had left us six years ago waving goodbye to his two children going north forever.

We arrived in Calgary in July 1963 during Stampede greeted by relatives wearing white cowboy hats and western wear. I felt like I had stepped onto a set from a Gene Autry movie.

I was more miserable than I had ever dreamed possible.

People did not speak the same; Danish accents mixed with Canadian Eh were hard to understand, customs and foods were different and it was so very cold.

I remember asking what happened to all of the trees. Had they been cut down?

I missed my Dad, Luella, house, and everything familiar.

The school year was torturous as teacher and classmates relentlessly mocked my accent. Standing at the front of the class, I would repeat a given sentence which gave rise to laughter, repeating it over and over until the pronunciation met the approval of the teacher.

I stood in front of a mirror each day practicing to sound like other kids and cried in misery each night while praying to go home.

I met Patti, a classmate living a few houses away who became a great friend teaching me to ice skate and toboggan fearlessly on every hill we could find during the long winter months. In summer we hiked through open fields and aspen groves to the river where we picnicked and floated on inner tubes down the lazy currents.

Our relatives kindly invited us for dinners serving wine with meals which stirred past fears of disaster. Initially I was horrified to watch mother drinking, as previous experience had only lead to sad endings in Tennessee.

I met new friends and began adjusting to our home.

Each fall a familiar box arrived from Tennessee packed with coats, boots and hats for winter. I continued writing letters to Dad and he remained determined to keep us in his life.

The three of us began carving out separate pathways for our future in Canada.

Dream Again?

During early teen years I began having a recurring dream that brought several questions about spirits into mind. The dream repeated the same frightening episode; a feeling of dying and exiting my body and I began to think it was a premonition or omen that something ominous was about to happen.

Anxiously I tested the waters asking friends about their dreams as the bothersome question lingered in my mind, "am I normal?"

I was a young woman dressed in peasant garb; a loose blouse that fastened by ties, a long full skirt and ankle boots. Long black wavy hair cascaded down my back as I was running down a hill of high grasses headed for the nearby woods. Women, children and men were screaming and running all around me. I looked over my shoulder towards the top of the hill and saw many attackers firing their weapons. As I turned around I felt an unbelievable pain hit my back causing me to fall to my knees. The pain was an intense torture; like nothing experienced before.

Lying in the field looking up at the sky I began slowly rising above my body. I felt weightless and free as I continued looking down upon the limp form, quite puzzled at the separation. There was no sound, just a sensation of peacefully floating, yet fully aware I was still alive even without a body.

The dream recurred several times and I pondered its meaning knowing nothing of past life, reincarnation or the soul when I was fifteen. The vision's meaning would not become clear until much later in life.

Peace Love Dove

Growing up in the sixties was an interesting challenge for society. Kids experimented with everything that was taboo in the past. Alcohol and drugs were easily accessible and for most it was a curiosity to taste forbidden fruit, but others turned it into a cultural revolution.

The sixties were exhilarating times of protest, change and incredible music. Freedom of expression had new meanings; life literally blossomed with the flower generation as new innovative ways rushed in.

It was a time that youth proclaimed change with a voice of majority. Love, Peace, and happiness were the key words to living in the sixties during the hippie groove and flower children movement.

Parents were unprepared as rebellious youths upset the applecart of life in homes everywhere and if they thought Elvis was a bad influence then their nightmares were just beginning.

It was easy to be swept up in the wave of long hair, psychedelic art, lyrical music and funky clothes, and it was fun. There were those who agreeably liked booze and drugs too much that grouped together for acceptance and support in ways not found at home.

The "Be-Ins and Love-Ins" were gatherings in parks filled with bands playing their messages, while dancing and fellowship spread harmony mantras of love and peace. Brilliant young minds sought ways to protest yet affect opinion with diplomatic gestures for swaying the masses towards peaceful enlightenment. Fraternities and sororities bonded by allegiance fuelled school spirit through basketball and football, identifying themselves by alpaca sweaters and penny loafers.

After the games everyone gathered at Glenmore Park where beer and cider flowed and mixed together with testosterone and adrenaline meant it was boisterous and wild. Most were sowing wild oats but some started to absorb this behavior into their personality. Depending on home life it sorted out who moved forward and who remained stuck on the wilder side of life, weeding out addictive personalities early on.

Habits turned into addictions for many who had problems with physical, sexual, or emotional abuse during teen years. They learned that booze or drugs gave the escape they needed, but none realized the dangers these crutches had in store for their futures.

Sadly, many who experimented with drugs and alcohol ended up as alcoholics, drug addicts, and disorders that required medical or psychological treatment, and most experienced failure in marriage or relationships.

I met Keith in grade twelve. He walked up to my locker and introduced himself by informing me I had two different shoes on. I looked down and was mortified that my shoes were indeed different. He was new to our school trying to meet friends so I invited him to an upcoming house party. He continued to call, show up with roses picked from the city park or drive me home after school. We dated off and on, but his rebellious attitude quickly became tiresome. He really gave his poor Dad a hard time and already by age seventeen decided it was his way or the highway regardless of age or authority.

Motherhood

I decided to take a year after high school to find a direction for my life. I spent several months with Dad in Tennessee enjoying time with grandmother and cousins over the summer. I contemplated staying, even accepting a job temporarily, but an invitation to visit friends in Florida eventually enticed me to move on. After touring through Florida from top to bottom I decided to hitch hike northward and met friends along the way who were exploring the land in the same manner. Youth Hostels were plentiful, housing freedom seekers travelling on a budget. After exchanging road stories a small group banded together for the return to Canada. Crossing through Buffalo and Niagara Falls was a beautiful welcoming sight viewing the magnitude of nature's power in action. Toronto's Yonge Street was the "groovy" place to be and the musical production of "Hair" spoke to those waving their banners high with long hair and matching fringed leather.

When the time came to move west the dreaded message passed on to all travelers was whatever you do don't get stuck in WA WA Ontario or else you may be on the side of the road for weeks. As I passed through I understood the meaning as it was just a big corner in the road lined with desperate youths hopeful that someone would take pity and offer a ride.

In those days it was encouraged and relatively safe to see your country on the road, occasionally meeting a weirdo, but generally uneventful. Sadly, those days of freedom are gone.

Arriving in Calgary I took a job at the Planetarium to save for my education but always felt restless, empty, and unsure of what I really wanted to do. The following summer I met my destiny when I became pregnant.

My plans changed drastically, focusing on saving money for the time I would be off from work.

Well, I was to be a Mom at age twenty, not at all what I had planned. When I could no longer hide my belly I packed up the car along with my dog Socrates and headed to the Okanogan Valley to wait out my time. I lived meagerly and felt lonely but luckily friends living an hour away came on weekends to play card games. Kimberlee was born by caesarian birth which at that time meant a hospital stay of two weeks. In those days if you were unwed it was mandatory for a social worker to assist in adoption papers in the event you chose not to keep your baby.

When I awoke after surgery the social worker informed me of a family that would be happy for my little girl. I was heavily drugged as he shoved a paper and held the pen in my hand. I felt a strong guidance from within and threw the pen and paper on the floor and managed "No". I was isolated from other mothers and nursery and every day for two weeks people from church, medical staff or social workers came by to talk about adoption.

When I could finally get out of bed I called Mom to say she had a lovely granddaughter. She took the first bus and arrived in Penticton to help me leave the hospital and get on my feet as I prepared for a new life.

Keith was overwhelmed this new little person was here to stay. We were both young and he still displayed the irresponsible side of his personality. I soon realized it was going to be myself and baby through this journey. I used my savings to stay at home with Kimberlee for the first year and began taking courses and working as a dental assistant into the second year, never receiving a penny of support from Keith. I had an opportunity to move to Vancouver and a great job as Kimberlee turned two.

My brother, living in Vancouver offered support, letting us live in his house for two months while away in Europe giving me time to get settled for my job and find daycare for Kimberlee.

Due to the moderate climate we skied, skated, hiked, played on beaches, picked our own fruits and veggies at the nearby U-pick farms, and walked in the rain everywhere. They were the best years of our life. Keith would show up now and again, while on vacation, to talk about trying to make things work, but was never interested in giving money for support or offering help. It was a meager existence for what little we had to live on but Kimberlee and I had a good life together.

The following year Keith bought a house in a small town in Alberta and wanted us to give it a shot by moving back and getting married. Maybe I was tired, deflated, worrying about Kimberlee having a father, missing my family; I really cannot remember why I agreed but looking back it was the worst mistake of my life. Within months after marrying, Keith began disappearing with his friends, drinking and staying out all night. We lived in a small country town very isolated and far from the city, family and friends. His job took him away from home for weeks at a time and with our lack of communication we started to disintegrate. After three years of living an isolated life and Keith's absence, I decided to instigate a move back to Calgary. After living apart for six months he applied for a different job in the oil and gas industry close to home and we decided to buy a house and focus on our family. Things went quite well for a time as we concentrated on providing our daughter with a stable home environment. We enjoyed vacations together and spent more time with our families and their children.

To ensure Kimberlee was in a better school district we built a home in a neighborhood we all felt happy to be in and life was good.

As time approached for University to start, Keith made sure Kimberlee had a better car, I worked three jobs to fill in some financial holes but life chugged along.

Keith continually drank each day throughout the years of our marriage. Sometimes it created extreme havoc other times it was manageable but it remained a wedge between us. There cannot be emotional truth with someone under influence of any substance. I lived a life of pretend and make believe.

I covered for Keith's shortcomings with business associates, friends and family. I did double duty at home making sure the "ginger bread house" looked warm and cozy. I gardened, baked, decorated, entertained with gourmet meals, dressed us in good clothing and presented a pretty picture to the outside world. I worked hard at my job and no one knew my personal suffering.

I remembered Grandma Minnie saying "never tell your family business to anyone; keep your own dirty laundry at home."

Home life was unpredictable and chaotic. I made dinner each night and left a plate covered on the stove for Keith to eat at whatever hour of the night he came home. Kimberlee would ask why I left dinner when he couldn't be bothered to join us, angry that the injustice of his actions did not suffer any consequence. My only answer was, I did not have vengeance in my heart.

I did not have an uninterrupted sleep for several years as each night he staggered and fell into our bed stinking of sour alcohol and stale smoke. At times he would pass out in his car until morning or the down stairs couch or just make it to the back porch and sleep under the stars. Eventually a bed went in the basement and whether he made it down or not was no longer my concern.

I attended AA meetings trying to gleam an understanding of this "disease", joined Al anon and went for individual counseling at Aadac but none seemed to help the slipping, deteriorating cycle of daily dysfunction.

A call came to pick Keith up from a night club as Kimberlee and I were just going to bed. She decided to come with me in the cold snowy night. We walked in and caught him red handed kissing and hanging over two other women. Kimberlee was mortified, I was beyond caring, and Keith was not fazed or embarrassed, saluting his friends through a chorus of cheering and hooting as we trundled out the door. Two nights later he left his company truck running because it was so cold but forgot to lock the door. Keith called with panic in his voice as he relayed his truck had been stolen, but somehow he managed to lie about the incident at work and it did not bring about change in him or his drinking.

In several areas of life including his job, things started to unravel. Clients began to complain of his boisterous demeanor and rude manners, and his reputation as unreliable added reasons to be turned over several times for advancement positions, accepting assignments in Russia that no one else wanted.

I used to prime him for upcoming special event days in advance by threats and consequences especially if they involved Kimberlee.

On our seventeenth anniversary we had reservations for dinner and tickets to a special event. Dressed and ready with hopeful anticipation, I tried to ignore the feeling that he was not coming home. Lighting the fireplace, playing favorite music I settled in for the night accepting I was alone when powerful emotion widened the hole in my heart of which poured pain and grief.

I begged Jesus to let me live the rest of my life in peace. I was tired and drained empty. As I sat sobbing, feeling heavy hearted, a sensation of arms wrapped around me and a voice told me to rest for as long as I needed.

Through tears and exhaustion I did not look nor did I care who was holding me; I was weak and weary and needed rest; the written promise was being met.

I do not know for how long I rested but eventually awareness of a familiar voice comforted me, telling me it was okay to move on, I had done all I could for Keith. The rest of his life would be by his own choices.

That same night while lying on the floor I found a machete underneath the couch. I went downstairs to look into a box that had previously caught my eye but had been distracted to check its contents. Inside were Biker vests of "color" and guns stored for one of his friends.

I remember staring and wondering how much more dysfunction would take place in my life. It woke me up to recent violent threats and black outs Keith was experiencing. I realized he had passed over into a dangerous and lethal dementia. Fears and reality clarified the direction I needed to follow for our safety.

I spoke to Kimberlee about a plan and emphasized the importance of not agitating him in any way. I made one last attempt of pleading with Keith to get help for his drinking as life could not continue this way. He told me he liked drinking, liked his lifestyle and had no plans for changing any time soon.

I began financially planning and preparing for living on our own, saving every penny. I was frightened of how unpredictable Keith's temper could be, so timing was crucial for removing what few possessions I could take. A day came with a two hour window of opportunity, fraught with anxiety and panic of being discovered.

As I left our home neighbors came to give me a hug and confessed they had known what was going on in our home for a long time and had been concerned for mine and Kimberlee's safety. Regretfully they witnessed Keith's drinking behavior on several occasions, and gave encouragement to be strong as life would get better.

We listed the house to sell and Keith began putting all other assets into an inaccessible off shore account.

After legal fees were paid I was back where I started twenty years before.

Life was full of despair and uncertainty as the lesson of loneliness and being alone hit full force. Could I have tried harder, would he eventually have changed? Nights were filled with grieving over mistakes and poor choices that led to this hurtful place in my heart. Gratefully my job demanded focus every minute of the day giving my tortured mind some respite.

I cannot mention all the years of torment and dysfunction that Kimberlee endured. I feel to interpret her feelings would be an injustice and misrepresentation to her.

I can say that my heart has been broken several times as a mother wanting happiness for my child only to see one disaster after the other chip away any stability or goodness that may have been possible. As we left our home and life with Keith behind us, we set out to pick up the broken pieces of our hearts, hoping to make a little "chicken salad" in our future.

The following passage is taken from a journal written in my early thirties. I include it for hope that another young Mother may find similarities in thoughts and know she is not alone.

Musings of a young Mother

I've often wondered about the personality of people involved in relationships of abuse whether it is substance or physical. Much has been written about the "Alcoholic" and movies depict their character for society to have a window pane view but what of the forgotten families. I believe there are personality similarities that can be found in people who bond with the alcoholic. We are deep thinkers and feelers of life's challenges and respond with great sensitivity. We also have an inner strength that some are drawn to especially those that subconsciously need to depend on it. Many who are alcohol dependent feel life's demands very deeply and are at times overwhelmed and seek escape. When living in an alcoholic relationship there are many stages the addict and family go through and one stage is isolation and secrecy from the outside world bringing with it loneliness and despair. Shyness comes from feeling embarrassed and mortified by the behaviors and daily dysfunction that comes from addiction. We try so hard to have the world see us as living a normal life but the realities are extremely abnormal. We are jugglers of truth having memories like an elephant so we don't screw up our lies. Families go through ongoing stages of grief every day. Children want their alcoholic parent to participate in their lives as they see other parents doing but know it is impossible and slowly grieve with each new turn down. Children become great artists at inventing stories or fabricating excuses for their parent and often feel so ashamed they rarely seek out a close friend to confide in. Children often feel they are the cause of their parent's illness and feel disliked by the parent who drinks to ignore them. It becomes a lifelong goal to seek their approval and love.

My daughter suffered from her father chipping away at her self-esteem and confidence. She looks into the mirror and does not like what she sees because there are permanent blindfolds in her mind of any beauty and brilliance. Always in the middle I struggle to create balance by nurturing and healing the destruction. I felt the need to be brutally honest even at a young and tender age about her father's problem hoping she understood he was the one that was sick.

I soothed and patched the mental bruises and emotional wounds for years.

It is difficult to understand what families go through with this disease unless they have lived through it themselves. During times I confessed our secrets to friends I observed blank stares and fidgeting while tactfully looking for an escape, disdain and anger for why I did not leave was clear upon their face. I usually felt worse about myself after the encounter, how I could be so dumb to let down my defense.

We lived forty miles outside the city in a town of two hundred and fifty people where my daughter at age five was free to play in a wonderful environment with playmates but I was forever lonely day after day, night after night.

My husband started as a binge drinker, I did not know what that was or recognize his drinking as a problem since he travelled away from home with his job.

In time he accepted a new job in the city that provided a company car and expense account for entertaining clients. There were many business lunches, golf games, dinners or drinks after work where he drank more and came home less.

My pattern of lying and covering for him if he was late for work due to a hangover was common. His binges increased in frequency creating anxiety in me of his whereabouts when he disappeared for days.

One summer evening while watching the glowing Northern lights I wallowed in a pity party, waiting as usual for him to return. We were to go for dinner with friends but I phoned with an excuse that he was working late. Moments later a call from a longtime friend raised my guard as she began asking many personal questions. My mind began backtracking, trying to remember which lie was which when she quietly said its okay, I know about the drinking. The rush of emotions was incredible ranging from defensive, hostile suspicion to grateful, humble relief. Freedom to admit I had lied for years and felt miserable with the deception, sorrow for not contributing more to our friendship; but more importantly the opportunity to speak openly about the festering spread of sickness through my family brought huge relief.

She suggested I attend an AL Anon meeting. At first, during meetings, all I could focus on was the enormous hurt as tears flowed like rivers choking back my words. Then emotions turned towards impatience and deep anger. I was appalled and frightened that I could feel such hate and the only good thing about this stage was that I no longer felt numb. I realized the ladies at Al Anon were much too complacent and calm for me at this stage because I was boiling and raging with a voice that was far from calm so I sought individual counseling for one and a half years. I created huge storms at home relentlessly pouring out my frustrations to my husband trying to get him to respond and agree to make some changes. I had a false sense of control, I was mad with little patience and demanded he co-operate in getting help. When he continued to drink and became more belligerent I decided I would show him how strongly I objected by moving back to the city. My daughter changed schools mid-year (I still cannot believe I did that) and I began a new job all within a week.

My husband became a total mess wanting to see me all of the time and finally said his life was so screwed up that he agreed to counseling. He showed a willingness to try and I felt that glowing hopefulness that we so often grasp onto as I agreed to try again. For a while it came together as we continued to seek help for repairing damage to our family but only long enough to secure his former life was restored.

"So where is Dad?" How many times have I been asked that question? It's a valid question, one that I surely feel I should have an answer to but seldom do. Her dad rarely comes home early enough for them to talk and she does not know the meaning of sitting around the table sharing a meal with him. In her younger years I could never rely on him for outings, always securing a sitter if I made plans with friends. How does my daughter look back on the past with her father? She doesn't or won't really tell me too much.

I know she thought he was always angry and feared him.

She was never comfortable being alone with him, and there was little respect between them. As she grew older and developed outside interests and friendships I don't think she really cared, more or less ignoring him as you would a fly on the wall.

The only times they communicated were during his reprimands or her requests. Perhaps the word to sum up their feelings is tolerated.

Many times we felt our lives were in danger when he was inebriated and refused to let me drive and the more I pushed the more anger arose, so we endured and prayed. A few times I simply refused to be in the car and he would stop along the highway and let us out. Walking was safer, hitch hiking not so much.

Observing the progression of alcoholism has certainly taken its toll, a part of me has died inside but maybe that is okay as I am less hysterical. The previous hope of sobriety has diminished; maybe my sense of reality is keener as I have learned to enjoy the good moments and wait out the bad.

I cannot deny the deep sense of loss though, and the pervasive sadness that sinks to depression.

The fighter instinct is not as predominant now but I am a survivor. I have moved into another stage where I would say apathy has set in solidly.

I no longer mention our marriage and home life, instead my pretense sounds falsely optimistic and happy when engaged in conversation. A smile is pasted on my face and it is so tiring to keep my eyebrows lifted and eyelids from drooping. I focus on pleasant thoughts and force myself every day into a mood of humor by thinking of funny experiences, changing the intonations of my voice to portray a happy countenance.

I smile in abundance, adopt bouncy body movements and laugh lightly at all opportunities. It is a betrayal of me ignoring my true emotional turbulence but everyone buys it. I struggle with my identity and self-worth searching each day for something of myself yet he casts a long shadow.

My daughter is pursuing her future at University so she can get out and away. Good for her!

I have noticed how few times we have shared harmony as a family, somewhat like a game of playing one against the other, two chummy that brow beat the third.

Lately we have discussed how immature her dad is, stuck somewhere in his early twenties, noticeable now as we have continued to mature where he stopped growing emotionally years ago.

It's strange to say you have lived with someone for fifteen years but don't know him. The alcoholic develops their own life elsewhere with people they can fool for some of the time and returns home with total disinterest and little participation. Some of our most explosive arguments have been when I pushed him to tell me where he had been.

An important rule to teach our children is never antagonizing someone who has been drinking heavily. We, ourselves, can use rational thinking in disputes but when under the influence of alcohol they are volatile and unpredictable. It is much better to walk away and deal with the issue at a sober moment and I did just that, feeling it was my right to let him know what had upset me the following morning.

I knew it grated his raw hung-over nerves but claimed a small revenge. It never made any difference mind you, but it helped me to regain self-respect. My daughter used to wonder why her dad was sometimes nicer when he drank.

The alcohol put him in a state where he thought people liked him and where he could like himself.

His drinking has moved to a new level and my feelings are of disgust and escape. He comes home very late at night or not for days and I am glad.

I walked through days as a zombie for years exhausted by his needs for talking at three in the morning on work nights or coming to bed in the middle of the night turning on the bedroom lights or flushing the toilet. I have a great dislike for him this morning. He comes upstairs bumping and banging around like a bull in a china shop and seems unsure of his acceptance in the clan after being away on a week-long binge using silly sarcasm to test the waters, so annoying. He is intruding on my peace which I have settled into during his absence. He starts to bully my daughter, he is so transparent and I am full of anger and spew out venom to everything he says.

He does not deserve kindness or conversation after such disregard and neglect.

I feel constant tension and impatience throughout my days now. I wake up feeling totally ill and lifeless, dizzy and aching all over like a bad flu every day.

The life force within me is weak and I struggle to focus on a goal to end my nightmare. There are far too many distractions and I have no defenses to the constant barrage destroying my peace.

I must remember that only I can improve my life, no one can do that for me and I must act very soon, just one step forward.

A New Beginning

John and I dated in high school and kept in contact with each other as good friends even though we had gone in separate ways and marriages. My divorce had finally gone through, and John had been divorced a year.

Life was a routine of work, eat and sleep. One evening I had a call from a realtor friend who said it was time to get out and meet people. I told her it was too soon but she insisted I join her at a hockey game and house party to meet her friends. Reluctantly, I went along and felt terribly uncomfortable both times, deciding I would rather watch movies at home.

John and I began spending more time together slowly rekindling feelings but realized we needed time to clear old baggage from painful past relationships.

In time we decided to rent a larger apartment, moved in together, and felt happy at finding joy in life once again. It was a cozy relaxing winter full of harmony and love, but as spring approached I began feeling a restless urge to have a home and garden again.

While heading out to visit mother I saw an open house sign and with impulsive action made a quick right turn winding through a neighborhood until I saw the house. I went inside and saw a lot of hard work to update the tired home but it was solidly built and the price was reachable. It struck me this was the house to buy and I couldn't really explain my feeling in any logical way.

Arriving at Mom's house, with excitement in my voice, I described the home and asked for her opinion. I phoned John and arranged for him to tour the home later the same day, and having a positive response went home and deliberated the pros and cons during the night.

My brother came the next day to talk about structural changes we knew had to be done for us to be comfortable.

In less than forty eight hours we found a home, placed an offer and wondered how this happened so quickly.

By July we moved into our new home and began the long hard job of renovating and settling into our lives. I felt at peace with the world having a place to call home once again.

Life was good; we had fun traveling, exploring, and rediscovering happiness we both had lost for such a long time. John and I were in Love again.

After living together for four years we decided to get married in our favorite place on the Big Island of Hawaii. I ordered Leis for our sunset ceremony and when they were unpacked the lady raised her eyebrows in surprise remarking our wedding leis were made in the old traditional way that only the elder lei makers knew and are rarely seen anymore. She said this was a sign of a special marriage. It was a lovely, emotional ceremony followed by an intimate dinner set in an outdoor garden illuminated by torches and candlelight. A musician came over with his acoustic guitar and serenaded us with (of course) the Hawaiian wedding song. It was a happy and love infatuated time we let ourselves drown in.

We both lost so much financially from our previous marriages, and it was not easy starting over at our age, but we were determined and had a plan. Within three years we managed major renovations to our home and bought a cabin on the west coast for a retreat. The cabin was surrounded by old cedars, spruce, and pine in a beautifully landscaped yard. There were several fruit trees, two that produced the most delicious figs I have tasted, but grew six to seven feet each year which was a pruning nightmare. Raccoons also savored the delicacies and squabbles often broke out as squirrels claimed their share.

John built raised garden beds for planting vegetables and herbs that yielded a bountiful harvest each fall. He built a Pergola to cover the outside fireplace and sitting area and I planted four varieties of grapes to grow as a canopy. The flower garden grew several varieties of heritage roses, and blue and purple hydrangeas that nestled around a red Japanese maple tree.

On a previous trip to Tennessee while standing in a cemetery with Dad speaking of the members of our family, John gathered sprouting acorns underneath an old Oak tree. We lovingly nursed them in pots throughout the winter and when they reached a decent height we planted them in the Pt. Roberts yard where they seemed to thrive.

The cabin needed TLC which we cheerfully went about redecorating and fixing. It was small, cozy and served its purpose well.

Pt. Roberts is a peninsula and within five minutes in any direction we were at the ocean. The bay, during low tide allowed a mile long walk out from shore into tide pools and the moist sea air was a welcomed rejuvenation from the dry Prairie.

John bought a small boat that we used for fishing, crabbing and day trips of sightseeing around the smaller islands of the west coast. Most of all we sat around our fire pit in the back yard under the stars or on the back deck in the rain listening to the owls in the forest and soaking up the peaceful quiet. We spent eleven summers there in great happiness.

Not so New

John's father struggled with health resulting from cancer and old scarring in his lungs. After a long courageous battle he finally passed on a very bitter cold stormy night in January 2005.

They say that people handle grief differently, but drinking was not what I had anticipated. I watched as John poured a full glass of scotch and asked, "Do you think that is a safe thing for you to do?" He replied he no longer had a problem with liquor. John had not drunk in ten years. What could I say? Nag and deny a man a drink after his father just passed away?

I quietly listened to the stories and comments each person needed to share but watched in amazement at the transformation of John's personality right before my eyes. I felt alarmed and my inner voice was screaming danger.

An old sleeping fear crept back into my heart and the dread of days ahead was all too familiar. It felt like a whirlpool sucking me downward into an uncontrollable void and past life. Inner peace vanished and storms returned with choppy seas and dreary horizons. No more mellow sunsets, rather long restless sleepless nights. My heart became frozen in its heartbeat, still tender, and not completely healed.

The next drink came on the day of the funeral and John told me not to worry it was only to see him through his grieving.

We left three days later to spend our anniversary in Hawaii. I could tell John was restless, not himself, and asked if he needed to talk about his father. He conned me to accept his drinking, to leave him be, that he was in control and this was not going to be a problem in our lives.

Over the next year John tried in vain to control his drinking by periodically abstaining from alcohol.

I noticed subtle changes in how we communicated and how he responded to me emotionally. He had jumped on the demon wagon for another ride, and once again I was living with Dr. Jekyll and Mr. Hyde.

The more I tried to talk about drinking as a problem in our lives the further we drifted apart. Intimacy suffered as John drifted more and more into the chemical changes taking place in his brain.

"God grant me the serenity to accept the things I cannot change."

In the second year of John's drinking I received news that Dad was dying from lung cancer. I made arrangements to fly down and spend some time with him before the chemo and radiation deteriorated his body. I flew down on July fourth watching a succession of fireworks over each city we flew over feeling heavy hearted about Dad and leaving John alone.

As usual my beloved south calmed my spirit as soon as I walked on the rich red soil. I was grateful sitting on the rocker listening for hours to memories, stories and songs from dad; back where all my bloodline and history began. I imagined those passed over sitting in the same place overlooking fields and trees of luminescent green lightning bugs wafting in the warmth of a southern night.

There is great comfort from ancestral lands, a peaceful knowledge and wonderment of familiar footsteps covering every path you have walked. Small moments offer glimpses of past generations embedded in genetic code, coursing through highways of vessels carrying our life blood. It's as though a spark ignites in our brain flashing glimpses of our ancestors; a sliding door of past and present seeing their struggles of living, loves of their lives, children, and their dreams.

I stayed for a week calling John each day and night never getting an answer or returned call from my messages. Dad kept asking why John did not call and I made one excuse after the other trying to remove extra worry for Dad. He really loved John and from our previous visits they had become good buds, but he knew something was wrong and felt I needed to get home. I promised to be back in a few months and tearful goodbyes left me drained and anxious at the situation I was leaving and what waited in Calgary.

I walked from customs and saw John's brother waiting to take me home. We both knew what was happening but chose to talk about my dad and Tennessee on the ride back. John did not answer the door and I did not have a key. Dennis tried to throw pebbles and call out to roust him. After a while John managed to open the door and let me in but Dennis wanted nothing to do with it and said good luck and left.

John had been drinking solidly the whole week I was away and was in terrible condition. His whole body was battered and bruised from the many falls trying to get to the bathroom and another drink.

He lost a lot of weight from not eating and burn marks from cigarettes marked the hardwood floor. He was lucky to be alive; we were lucky to still have our home.

The poor canaries were neglected and desperate for nurturing care. Well, here I was back into alcoholism at its very worst. I had come full circle reliving my nightmare once again only with a different face.

I sat on the front porch distraught with sadness for dad, present circumstances and feeling loss coming in all directions.

Time Marches On

Mother was diagnosed with Benson's syndrome in 1998. It is a progressive degenerative condition affecting the back section of the brain responsible for visual interpretation. The damage to brain cells leads to cell death and atrophy of the posterior cortical regions hence the name Posterior Cortical Atrophy, the medical name given. The death of brain cells is accompanied by toxic proteins, amyloid and tau that form plaques and tangles. PCA is a rare condition believed to affect two percent of persons with typical Alzheimer disease. The effects of PCA upon behavior, thought processes and skills of individuals are different. The most common problem first noticed is with vision and an individual may see an optician at first thinking their eyes are the problem. The affected brain cannot interpret the information received from the person's eyes. Difficulties recognizing objects in pictures, faces, decline in spatial awareness such as descending stairs, reading certain types of text, increased sensitivity to bright light or perceiving objects having an unusual color are noticeable signs. Developing difficulties with handwriting, remembering the shape of letters or numbers, dealing with money, problems with dressing are a few of encountered frustrations. PCA tends to affect people at an earlier age than Alzheimer's disease, with individuals being in their mid – fifties or sixties. Due to visual oddities appearing first it may take three or more years to get a diagnosis from a neurologist after the onset of symptoms. As the disease progresses, word finding, short term memory along with general cognitive functions become affected. The duration of PCA condition is poorly understood suggesting a time line of ten to twelve years but many including mother who is going on twenty years (including time before diagnosis) carry on for much longer.

Individuals struggle with a loss of independence as their ability to perform the basic activities of daily living is compromised and they can no longer enjoy previous hobbies. This leads to depression, irritability, frustration and a loss of self-confidence. In the advanced stages of PCA there is still awareness to surroundings and daily routine and although impaired, verbal skills are present which sets PCA apart from most dementias and Alzheimer's disease.

It is emotionally, physically, mentally heart wrenching and exhausting for family who assist their loved one through the years of decline. I look back at pictures of Mom and mourn over the loss of this vibrant lovely woman who loved life zestfully and after years of PCA ravaging her brain hardly recognize the person I love so dearly.

After returning from Tennessee I wanted to talk about the sad struggle her former husband was going through, but still hanging on to bitterness from divorce fifty years ago would not allow her to shift angry emotions towards compassion.

The disease turned her inward; self-centered towards life. Every discussion related back to her circumstances as the ability for empathy for the woes of others was lost. It was painful especially when you needed a listening, caring ear that only a mother can provide. Over the years I tried reaching out for advice or support from mother telling her of the dysfunctional incidents occurring in my marriage with Keith. It was just not in her to be forthcoming with helpful advice in any way. By self-admission if problems were too difficult she minimized their significance or simply refused to face them as an Ostrich does when it sticks its head in a hole.

The mother daughter relationship had often been difficult throughout our lives, strained by our different personalities and views on life.

I made a conscious choice to distance myself emotionally as much as possible, aware of the unhealthy mental state our exchange often left me in.

Sadly, her connection to the outside world fell on my shoulders as she lost touch with former friendships which further tested our patience and commitment for the long road ahead.

In the early stages of PCA Mom was retired, lived outside the city limit with no access to buses, and alone all day while the rest of us worked. We all dedicated time for activities with Mom each week but her unrest and boredom were stifling.

During this time I broke my leg in two places and after a two week recovery needed to get back to work but was unable to drive. Most days I commuted by taxi but one day Mom offered to pick me up and drive me home. I knew she had always been a tentative driver but this time was downright frightening as we zoomed through stop signs and yellow lights. Soon after, another potentially serious incident took place while driving and within the next few months she slid off the road into a ditch as daylight was fading.

After seeing several doctors and specialists it was determined she could no longer drive. Mom could not accept the test results bitterly insisting she wanted a second opinion and new eye glasses to fix the problem. An Ophthalmologist determined that cataract surgery and glasses may improve her sight but when the procedure failed to bring satisfaction Mom was livid with her health care providers.

Over time we finally realized rational problem solving was compromised rendering her incapable of understanding or accepting she had a medical condition. Her inability to realize she has a brain malfunction has been the hardest to cope with for the entire family as denial leads her towards anger and confusion with best laid intentions running amuck.

When a parent begins to slip into any form of mental disorder family members react with many types of emotion. Mother's personality was changing right before our eyes faster than we could adjust and her frustrations were vented on anyone within reach.

As cognitive disability became more noticeable, our frantic efforts to bring her contact with the outside world were met with extreme resistance.

Her mind dwelled in conspiracy that we were going behind her back and mistook help as personal interference, classifying her incapable of looking after her life. She felt insulted and outraged we were interfering in her life, yet, insisted it was my duty as I was the daughter and that is what daughter's do. I knew this was the fearful side of her personality speaking and tried not to let personal emotion over ride her desperate plea.

Her fears and worries attached to aging were a constant plague to her youthful mind that searched endlessly for ways to enjoy life and retain a youthful appearance.

I loved how spontaneous her spirit responded to suggestions of new places and things to explore with girlish excitement and this side of her personality never ceased with age or dementia. "I feel young and I love Life!" were words I heard often and believe this attitude is Mom's fountain of youth.

As deterioration in the brain progressed her personality and capabilities regressed. John felt more burdened with day to day chores as Mom could no longer see, even though in her own mind she continued to maintain her housework.

When John met Dyma she had a great job, respectable home, and youthful appearance. He was struggling financially, and not happy as a teacher took a job with the City of Calgary where they met but soon discovered it was not the career he hoped for. During the early years they were together John was clear he did not want to get married and I heard this many times from mother and knew it hurt her deeply. It was another reason why she worried about a younger appearance due to their difference in age.

They had a good life together, camping, fishing and entertaining friends frequently. John's passion for flying meant the weekends during summer were dedicated to gliding and parties with other pilots and their wives.

During the Winter Olympics in Calgary, they drove by a two acre parcel for sale and after discussing their plans decided to buy the land, have Dan design a home and begin the process of building their dream.

They worked hard together landscaping and turning their country estate into a beautiful retreat to retire and enjoy the latter years of life and we were happy their wishes had come true. Within a couple of years Dyma retired to home life enjoying simple pleasures of gardening and hobbies but John had several years of work left before retirement which interrupted the travel and vacation plans Dyma had hoped for. Friendships from work drifted apart, and loneliness set in. I gave encouragement to join groups, or enroll in courses which met resistance each time.

Mom's bizarre accusations and suspicions directed towards women, even family members coming into the home began to surface as her mind slipped into the past of extramarital affairs, jealousies and insecurity.

We absolutely needed to discuss her needs, health care, and finances so the paranoid outbursts threw us into unknown territory adding unneeded stress to life.

Even though my husband John was present during some episodes, only deep seated fears of deception were exposed from her mind.

Dementia had trapped her in the past reliving the unfaithful days of marriage.

John fell further into depression, anxiety and despair feeling trapped in a life he no longer wanted.

Little information was available for Posterior Cortical Atrophy as it is rare worldwide and comparisons to Alzheimer disease are inaccurate. Medications that helped Alzheimer patients presented extreme adverse reactions, agitating Mom into uncontrollable behaviors. Blindness is inevitable with PCA as the brain can no longer decipher what a person sees even if their eyesight is perfect. Coupled with memory loss their world narrows unless someone is willing to sit down and draw them out with one on one conversation. TV and reading is lost, hobbies using sight are gone and if they have always been an active person, life suddenly becomes an anguished disappointment. Independence is taken away which is so difficult for any person to lose but the issue of safety becomes paramount. Walking outside, assistance with bathing and dressing means that someone is always taking away your most private moments. As a family we have suffered along with Mom trying to manage a disease with no help from the medical profession who admittedly says there is little that can be done other than sedating her into oblivion. There is no care facility prepared to provide the level of attention Mom requires and we are left juggling our lives alongside with caregivers who are also at odds with managing this incomparable disorder.

After living with the disorder for twelve years Mom still cannot understand there is anything wrong with her, and instead determines it is the fault of someone or something else for common mishaps. The bizarre part is that she adamantly claims to see everything perfectly which leaves us shaking our head at how to manage safety with a respectful distance.

There are days of lucidity and rationality and our response of care is likened to the brakes and accelerator of a car.

Although progression of PCA is slower than Alzheimer disease the decline does continue with adjustments made in daily life on a regular basis.

Again because of her independent personality each change was met with denial and refusal to acknowledge that outside help was necessary. A firm hand of saying this is just the way it will be was met with erratic anger that fueled physical and emotional outbursts causing more harm than good so we quickly learned to do what needed to be done in a quiet fashion.

Finding a support group for discussing techniques for managing PCA was non-existent eleven years ago.

The internet has brought together a small worldwide group that shares stories providing small inklings of information and perhaps empathy from others walking the same road.

Baby boomers are labeled the "Sandwich generation" as we barely become empty nesters before jumping back into caregiving roles for parents now living longer. There is a good reason why we have our children at a younger age as energy required for looking after grandchildren or parents does not have the same quality and expires quicker.

The strain on marriages and one's own health is immense but the only question left to ask is what else can you do?

You cannot simply discard or push aside a human being just because they are elderly and disabled.

Everyone that faces dementia with parents must dig deep within themselves and consider many things about their loved one before sending them away into a stranger's hands.

Observing mother's personality and knowing how she lived her life in younger years gave me insight into the direction for her care.

For instance she was never a group activity person and loved her time alone in nature either walking or sitting listening to the birds. She was basically a shy person finding it difficult to speak to others unless someone approached her first.

She wanted to be active socially and could be the instigator but not the planner or action taker. Her whole life revolved around family so placing her in public groups made her fearful and insecure. Expecting her to adjust to a completely foreign way of life with lost cognitive function was one thing but to ignore her personality was a recipe for disaster. The person inside is still the same even though their outer personality presents itself in unusual ways.

We all continue trying to fill the cup for Mom's happiness and at age ninety two we can barely keep up to her tireless search to relieve the boredom she feels each day. Dinner and dancing or the mention of a party lifts her spirit.

It is a fine line of balance lying somewhere between walking on egg shells and treading water when a parent experiences mental decline to tactfully step in and help respectfully.

The decline each year has been sad to witness and frustrating beyond all strength. In the early stages of the disease, John did not know which direction to take; could not make any decisions for change, so remained in the house and acreage that was burdensome to maintain.

Although I understood Mom's negativity and defensive actions as being fearful of losing independence, it hindered possibilities for improving her life. Introducing a woman companion and housekeeper has been a war like negotiation.

Always a private person, Mom is now forced into having caregivers come into her home each day and feels assaulted and intruded upon and truly I understand her despair.

John has reached his limit saying no outside help brings relief to his anguished mind.

There are situations we can find ourselves feeling mentally and emotionally stuck and for some making a change can be more terrifying than remaining in what is familiar.

Decision making has never been one of John's strengths. I know John wants to be rescued and have Dan and I make the decision that Mom go to a care facility but we have said they are partners and he must be involved in this life altering decision.

Statistics show we are entering into an age of brain related disorders in unprecedented numbers and our care facilities are only prepared to place individuals under the same kind of treatment. When a person cannot comply with the one treatment fits all scenarios the only recourse is to heavily sedate them to a bed ridden state. This is a very sad truth and completely unnecessary with kinder alternatives available and I know there are others out there that feel the same way. I have a vision for a better way, do you?

Like the Emperor's new clothes the personality is the clothing our soul wears to navigate through life. Treating the illusions/delusions of mental disorders by responding to the personality of someone with diminished cognitive function will yield more positive results and mental comfort than rigid conformity. It is their world that we must enter and abandon our thinking of what we think they need to enhance what stage the person with dementia is living presently. Supporting the desires of the personality is more humane than forcing immense change and numbing drugs. As a person's world narrows due to dementia they are left with fewer mental and emotional attachments or recognitions, so the ones that remain are vital to happiness and comfort. For example, Mothers happy memories from parties and dancing evoke emotional pleasure. At times serving a drink of iced tea is perceived as an alcoholic beverage releasing a spirit of laughter, conversation and uncanny youthful and pleasurable response.

Supporting her emotion with music and a dance around the room enhances her moments of joy.

I consciously focus a loving energy within my field in Mom's presence; periodically placing both hands on her body always observing the immediate response to touch. Sometimes I never speak a word but she will say hi Linda with a huge smile.

I conclude that although mother has limited vision her ability to read energy fields through subconscious mechanisms draw her closer to familiar warmth even before physical touching occurs. In a room of people she may approach a stranger but after a moment move away going from one to the other until with no words spoken recognizes a familiar energy and links her arm together. Her body language expresses relaxed comfort.

An intention to influence current ways of "handling" dementia through personality discovery for custom care approach will hopefully assist those souls who are ending their journey to depart in states of pleasurable peace and fulfillment rather than isolation and longing.

Assisting our elderly family members is an all-consuming commitment, for we desperately want them to be happy, healthy and safe.

Farewell

The months following dad's diagnosis were full of anguish and despair. Heartstrings pulled from afar and an overwhelming desire to help care for a loved one when you cannot be present is heartbreaking. Dan and I took turns flying down to Tennessee spending time with Dad and accompanying him to the many chemo, radiation and doctor visits. He was incredibly brave and strong putting his life and faith into the hands of doctors and medicine all the while his poor body was poisoned and burned.

I flew down for my last visit in March as did Dan and by the middle of April we received word he would likely pass within twenty four hours. Dan and I quickly made the decision to be with him as he left this world rather than wait for his funeral. We arrived the next morning and he was waiting. Although he was too weak to speak, he managed to whisper as we sat with him through his last days and nights.

On Dad's last day I sensed he was agitated and locked away from words could only communicate with his eyes.

It has always been my rule not to interfere or enter another's energy field unless asked but I desperately wanted to ease dad's anxiety. I told Dan not to let anyone come into the room as I began channeling and reading his body. My hands were placed on his head where I felt the most unrest and immediately knew he was worried if God and heaven were really waiting and if he was going to rejoin his beloved mother. He had concerns around everyone he was leaving behind knowing his journey was coming to an end. All of a sudden he opened his eyes looking intently into mine and with a clear voice said "hands are too hot".

I looked down at dad where my hands had been and saw red imprints beaded up with dripping sweat.

I was bothered by interfering with a sacred process a soul journeys through a body, however after relating dad's thoughts to Dan we addressed his concerns confirming everything would be okay here on earth and for him to stay close to his lifelong beliefs of heaven. His body relaxed as he began the final hours of his journey. He managed to say he was going home tonight, then hesitated and said well, maybe in the morning.

Dad's loved ones were with him sharing love and comfort, sobbing pain of loss as we watched him exhale his last breath. True to his teasing humor as I looked up at the clock it was five minutes past midnight.

A chapter of life closed forever in Tennessee. Never again would I hear unconditional acceptance and love from a voice that brought balance to life.

Dad was the last generation to live and die in the valley of his forefathers. We flew back to Calgary after saying goodbye to our childhood home, both knowing we would never be back again.

Yearning never ceases to wander in dreams seeking
A replenished soul nurtured in my beloved South.

For a heart knowing her secrets feels a land of gentle harmony and grace; a garden to replenish and restore from long winters.

Balmy nights of earthly musk,
Fireflies in symphony of meditative crickets,
Stir the mind in dreamy thoughts of peaceful bliss.

Muddy rivers; lazy giants caressing grassy banks of willows and moss draped ancient oaks, flirt with gentle breezes.

Heady scents of wisteria and magnolia swirl in romance of young lovers, embraced, beguiled in shadows of an incandescent moon.

Goodbye

I arrived to a familiar seen with anger and resentment fuelling reactions to John's inebriated stupor. It will take time and forgiveness for not being present and supportive during this time of grief. We were to fly out the next morning to Palm Springs for a week of vacation arranged eight months prior. John was hung over and kept saying he could not make it but I was having none of it. I forced him to pull himself together for the four hour journey saying he could sleep for the next week for all I care but we were going to be on that plane no matter what. I was emotionally drained and physically exhausted and had not slept for thirty six hours.

I chose a spa in Palm Springs with natural hot spring mineral waters known for its healing properties. It was one of the original springs in the area that has been Native American land for as long as written records.

While soaking in a private mineral bath a vision that felt like a gift from the spiritual world washed through me. Leaving the bath I mentioned to an attendant my strange dream and she smiled giving me a hug and told me these are powerful healing waters and I must have needed a healing from their ancestors. She told others working there of my visions and as I was leaving they each gave me a hug and blessing.

The following was channeled while in the healing waters of Palm Springs April 2008.

Relaxed and mentally drifting, a picture appeared of how this sight once looked. The spring was a gathering place for ceremonies during which men wore beaded leather and feathered head gear. A large number of men stood in a semi-circle around the spring with their backs facing the water, gazing upward with arms raised above their heads lowly chanting. The women and children sat on the edge softly humming, patting hands in rhythm on the sand while gazing into the water. It felt like they were summoning a very powerful energy.

A multi petal flower resembling a lotus floated above the solar plexus chakra in golden colored light, spiritual, wise and peaceful. The light emanating from the flower was bright, pearlescent rays. As life unfolds so do the petals of the flower as a soul evolves in its journey towards spiritual wholeness. As each petal unfolds rays of light emerge until the center becomes a brilliant beam connecting us to the universe.

Mother earth's extended hands emerged from the depths of the sea cupping a body inside a semi bubble, rising towards the sun and heavens. A brilliant rainbow reflected colors of energy centers, "As above, so below" a reminder that heaven is on earth if we choose to open our hearts and minds to love and joy.

It was a week spent in grieving for the loss of my father and a week of sobriety for John. We each healed a little bit in our own way.

Sad Ending

Within a few days after returning from Palm Springs Kimberlee called to say her dad was in the hospital and had been given little hope of survival.

Alcohol had ravaged his body, scarring his liver and corroded his portal artery. He would never recover unless he received a liver transplant but must be clean and sober for a length of time to even be considered and time was running out. Medicine could do nothing more than keep him comfortable during the days he spent in a hospice.

Kimberlee had a two year old, an infant, and the world of Keith's messy affairs upon her shoulders.

Admittedly I was still reeling with the recent passing of my own father and the last drinking episode with John but offered help in any way she needed. I was puzzled by her actions; even though help was offered, she seemed to need the emotion of going through her father's passing as a single child, alone. I witnessed her need to control which only fed the drama she became so comfortable with throughout her life.

I encouraged her to allow others to assist, that Keith had been a part of my life for twenty three years and of course I would be there in this time of need.

He had sisters, a brother, father and a girlfriend who could help but she would not delegate any of it, feeling it was her cross to bear.

I decided to visit Keith in the hospital and immediately felt an uneasy hesitance from Kimberlee.

I was dumfounded, but realized Keith may have expressed the ever lingering bitterness of bruised pride.

After contemplating my intentions I decided as an act of human compassion what could be so wrong in saying goodbye to the father of my child no matter how many resentments we carried?

When I arrived at the hospital Kimberlee, Keith's sister and friend were there waiting. Did they think I was going to create a scene? They all seemed nervous and understandably protective but I calmly said it would be okay.

Keith drifted in and out of consciousness as I spoke of the positive memories of our life. I commented on realizing he may not have wanted me to visit when he clearly said "why would you say that?" I knew then it was okay that I had come, and although he may not remember the visit, needed him to hear whatever was between us was forgiven.

I prayed for his troubled soul and said goodbye.

When I walked out the energy surrounding those waiting was oppressive, competitive, and negative, sparking with ego and will power and I felt relieved not to be involved.

As Keith lay dying, one of his best friends and best man at our wedding died in a car accident in Victoria. They were born on the same day, year and hour and here they were both leaving this world in the same year.

The day Keith passed Kimberlee did not call and receiving the news from her husband, asked if they would let me know when and where the service would take place as our family wanted to support Kimberlee and offer condolences to Keith's family.

Receiving no call I read Keith's obituary finding details of the memorial and during the service a slide show reflected Keith's life and people who had been a part of it and nowhere was there a photo of us as a family.

It was as though twenty three years of life had never existed.

Throughout the next year John's drinking became a steady routine. He arose later each morning for work and came home earlier starting his "cocktail hour" sooner. We saw each other for dinner but right after the meal he went upstairs for his nap that increased from thirty minutes to two hours. He got up around nine thirty for half an hour then by ten he was out for the night. We had no life together socially because John became anxious if he could not be home in the afternoon for happy hour.

Physically he developed high blood pressure, digestive problems and chronic coughing, sleep apnea, liver weakness, weight gain and redness to his complexion. His behavior was agitated, anxious, short tempered and impatient.

He distanced himself from emotional issues from family and work and day to day routine chores became an inconvenience. He did not participate in life.

Our winter vacation planned together with family was used as an opportunity to go wild with cheap liquor in Honduras. I was stunned at the amount he drank and still managed to wake up the next day.

Between the dysfunction of mother and John it was an emotional drain and strain throughout the entire vacation.

I fell deeper into despair as I witnessed the avalanche of John's life knowing we were both powerless to the monster within.

The decision to sell our cabin in Point Roberts was made in spring after a brief trip out to the coast. John was not interested in doing the necessary maintenance required and I knew I could not handle it on my own so after discussing the option of selling, within a month we listed and six weeks later our little place sold.

A quick possession request meant a scramble to organize the long twelve hour drive and time off work.

We needed a few days to pack personal belongings and wrap up business transactions but each day the new owners came to ask questions and show friends their new possession leaving us no time to relax and say goodbye to our little place.

Feeling somewhat deflated, instead of vacationing in the Okanagan we both agreed to drive home quickly. John and I were looking forward to enjoying our backyard and summertime in Calgary.

His mother was in a battle with liver cancer and mine needed assistance so we both felt the need to be close to home.

We decided to buy a hot tub and put an outdoor fireplace in the back yard to enjoy cooler evenings a bit longer and generally a calm routine settled between us as we enjoyed the warm summer days of August.

Dear Ryan

On Sunday August 16, 2009 the family gathered for dinner at a local Thai food restaurant to say goodbye to Dan who was heading to New Mexico for a holiday then down to Roatan for business.

We discussed what everyone was doing and Dan brought us up to date with Ryan's latest news and bizarre marriage to Jasmine Fiore whom none of us had met. It was a whirlwind of dating fast forwarded into marriage in the little white chapel in Vegas. It did not seem to fit Ryan's character sending up red flags and alarm bells. Dan shook his head with worry about their relationship as Ryan told him Jasmine would disappear for two or three days at a time never telling him where she was.

Ryan worried about her and frequently called Jasmine's mother or friends to ask if they had been in contact with her. She always returned but defensively objected to his questions of her whereabouts.

Back in January 2009, Ryan met a person involved with casting an upcoming reality show called Megan wants to be a Millionaire. She was convinced Ryan would fit the role and by February he was filming and we were excited to see what the show was all about. Dan had spoken with Ryan periodically to make sure he was alright but could not release any details other than to say he was in the number two spot from winning. It seemed like a fun experience that Ryan would enjoy because he had always been such a ham.

Since he was a little boy he would impersonate celebrities while he and Dan kibitzed back and forth. Our family used to joke around suggesting he should go into acting.

His combination of quick wit and facial expressions were hilarious.

Ryan was such a beautiful little boy with large warm brown eyes and hair. He always had an infectious laugh and kept us all busy with his energy.

We were a close family celebrating every holiday and birthday together, playing games, skiing, golfing and supportive in each other's endeavors.

Ryan was an amazing swimmer, winning several competitions, but was successful standing out in most things he attempted during his youthful years. He did well in school and was a commercial pilot for a time. As the real estate boom continued in Calgary he decided to learn more about land development and threw himself into a successful career partnering with his dad for design and urban development. We were so proud of him and he seemed happy and content.

It was never hard to read Ryan; he was an open book never holding back feelings when sharing the ups and downs of life's experiences. Even through all of his bravado I always saw the warm hearted young man. He was the first to ask where Christmas, or Thanksgiving dinner would be held, loving the family traditions from childhood. When walking through the front door he smiled from ear to ear, hugging us with greetings like "how is my little auntie" or "nana it's good to see you".

Ryan was the first to propose a toast at dinner and our lively conversations ranged in topics from galaxies to diapers. If things got too serious Ryan would jump in with some explanative in impersonator style and crack us into peals of laughter.

Calgary's boom went bust and one of the first areas to show a downslide was real estate, particularly new home construction. Ryan turned to selling commercial real estate but it was lean and mean times.

When the reality show proposal came about he jumped for it as an opportunity to make some money during the current dry spell.

Participating in a reality show is a grueling experience when sequestered in a home with strangers under the constant eyes of a camera for several weeks. Many have undergone psychological debriefing and experience depression after completing the production. You live in an unreal environment that is tense, competitive and based on deceptions.

After filming the show, Ryan spent time in Las Vegas where he met Jasmine and to our shock and surprise revealed they were married, after only knowing each other a short time.

They were together for a month when Ryan was chosen to be a contestant in another reality show to be filmed in Mexico, again sequestered for six weeks.

Jasmine took this opportunity to vacation nearby with a girl friend and former boyfriend.

When Ryan completed filming the show he returned to Las Vegas to be with Jasmine but it was a bumpy marriage from the beginning; two people completely ill matched. There were frequent squabbles over money as Jasmine believed Ryan to be wealthy when they met. Ryan disclosed to a friend that Jasmine had been involved with illegal drugs and wanted to get out from that way of life.

She confessed she was paid a lot of money "for business" flying to Cabo San Lucas for days at a time. She told Ryan that in the past, most of her money had come from illegal drugs, and as Ryan continued to learn how deeply entrenched Jasmine was he agreed they needed a new beginning and the decision was made to move to Los Angeles.

Jasmine however, kept her connections in Las Vegas and continued to disappear for several days at a time.

Ryan talked with his Dad and Mom about her strange behavior and they begged him to get out. He insisted he wanted to help her break away from the underground lifestyle and that he had fallen in love with her.

Ryan flew back to Calgary for a quick trip to sell his home and clean up some business and Dan again tried to convince him to leave Jasmine that she was treating him badly and the relationship couldn't last. Jasmine herself talked about annulment but regretfully did not pursue it.

While partying around a pool in Las Vegas Jasmine displayed flirtatious behavior with other men and a former boyfriend. They had been drinking and she was kissing her former friend when Ryan came over and said it was time to go.

Jasmine made a scene yelling and swearing and Ryan pushed her into the pool, joking she needed to cool off. Jasmine became angry and charged him with assault.

Ryan was put in jail for two days because he pushed her into the pool.

After his release the dust settled and they were back together weathering stormy days that new relationships bring. At times their relationship was tumultuous as will powers collided and personalities clashed; other moments they found happiness in each other's company.

We felt completely helpless so far away; he would not listen to any advice and the entire family felt he was in over his head but had no idea of the dangerous people he had become involved with. After all, Ryan was thirty two, a man to handle his own life.

Jasmine pressured Ryan about money and was angry when she realized he was not the millionaire she had set her sights on. She taunted him by telling stories of wealthy men she met while affiliated with functions at the playboy club and expressed her dates were very generous. She quoted names of "influential, powerful men" she dated and drove a Lamborghini when they met explaining it was a friend's car.

Ryan wanted to buy Jasmine the expensive clothes and jewelry she craved, frequenting boutiques that filled the void of happiness briefly.

It was decided to try their luck at gambling and through Jasmines connections they were invited to some high stakes gambling parties and Ryan was like a baby swimming in a shark tank. He had never been exposed to this element of society and did not have the street smarts to navigate in that environment. Jasmine would openly ridicule Ryan in public, cruelly attacking his faults but in his blindness he continued to think he could save her from this hardened side of her nature.

He began telling some of her acquaintances that "Jasmine wanted out" and he was going to help her.

Alone, she told Ryan she wanted to settle down with a quiet life, but later panic would return and she became desperate, fearing Ryan could not provide her with the money and lifestyle she wanted. Jasmine felt she had a small window of time and opportunity for youth and appearance to manipulate the world of money in her favor. Indeed they both were caught in a web of shallow beliefs and needs.

Ryan had an upcoming visa hearing forcing him to return to Canada and wanted Jasmine to accompany him. Jasmine began telling friends she was taking a trip north and days before they were to leave an invitation came to a party in San Diego that Jasmine insisted they attend.

On Tuesday morning August eighteen, I received a phone call from a local television station asking if I was related to Ryan Jenkins. I said yes I was his aunt and asked why they were calling.

The person confirmed my relationship twice and I asked if this call had anything to do with Ryan appearing on the reality show "Megan wants a Millionaire." She asked if I had been watching the developing news story about Ryan and Jasmine Fiore and I confessed I had missed the news cast last night.

She began asking more questions about Ryan and I said, "You know I think I will go online to read the newspaper before I answer any more questions." Before I had a chance to read the paper, another call came from the station, this time apologizing for "the shock" of the unfolding story. I was bewildered as they spoke of an investigation in the disappearance of Ryan's girlfriend Jasmine.

My heart stopped as I felt a powerful wave of energy engulfing my body. It was so intense I can only describe it as being enveloped in a denser jelly like substance immediately feeling heavier.

It was as though I passed through a different dimension; a wall of darker, heavier, dull colored vibration around me.

I could hardly breathe as the impact and intensity of what was unfolding consumed me even before it completely unfurled into the world.

When Jasmine's body was discovered the media turned its attention on Ryan painting him as a monster. Over the next few days as the media storm hit frenzied proportions I knew Ryan would never survive to tell the true story. He was a gentle soul and would be torn apart from the rallied anger and misconceptions of his intentions.

Ryan himself had been saved and brought into the fold of Jesus eleven years ago and knew all too well the joy of having a second chance. He truly did love Jasmine and wanted to help her find a better life.

I tried desperately to reach my brother feeling somehow at all costs we would have to protect Ryan until time allowed some truths to surface, but with hundreds of calls and his state of high anxiety he initially did not recognize my number. When we finally connected he said only that Ryan was safe.

We received calls day and night from media personnel from all areas of the U.S and Canada.

We had no peace for our suffering and state of shock that permeated our lives. Our phone calls were monitored and we were under surveillance wherever we went. The hot tub we had previously ordered arrived in a moving van and as soon as the truck parked in front of the house two plain clothes men appeared out of nowhere to speak with the driver. As we walked out to see what was going on they asked if we were moving and I sarcastically asked who wanted to know. They stood across the street observing the unloading process and waited until the truck closed its doors and drove away.

A nationwide manhunt was declared for Ryan as the prime suspect for Jasmine's murder as he drove northward to Canada. He heard the news by talking with family and decided to abandon his car and make his way from Blaine to Point Roberts, a small peninsula border crossing. There he walked across and found his way into Vancouver Canada. Media reported daily with a frenzied mob mentality that intensified with each passing hour. There was complete confusion within the family as we were all immobilized from fear helplessly hoping he would make contact. A plan was made for Ryan to meet with a lawyer who would accompany him as he turned himself over to authorities but then with no last phone call or written word it was over, Ryan was gone.

Ryan chose to spend his last days in a small town called Hope, indicative of his hope that a miracle could bring truth to his tattered beliefs in a system that had failed him. Dan said "I think in his loneliness and despair he simply gave up."

I felt Ryan's pain, despair, fear, and loneliness; I felt it all, and for hours could not get off the floor sobbing helplessly throughout the night.

The following day Dan called to confirm that Ryan was gone, he had taken his own life during the night, and the hole in the blueprint of all our lives was permanent.

Our hearts were broken.

We were traumatized as we helplessly watched a nation of strangers destroy the precious person we dearly loved. Each piece of Ryan's life that could be used against him was manipulated into a picture of unimaginable horrors. It was a lynch mob mentality and that is what killed Ryan. Throughout the entire horrifying ordeal Dan did not get a chance to see or talk to his son. In the last three days of his life Ryan knew he could not call nor email his Mom or Dad in order to protect them. Ryan would have known what lay ahead and knew the world would never listen. With bail set at ten million, money that no one had, it would be years of jail and a lengthy trial with pre-determined public verdict. Following the pool incident with Jasmine, Ryan declared to his Dad "I cannot spend another day in jail; not one more day; I would rather die." It was a foretelling of the tragic events to unfold later.

To this day there has never been any forensic evidence linking Ryan to Jasmine's death; only circumstantial.

Jasmine's body was found on August fifteen at seven A.M. and the Orange County Coroner's Office reported the time of death was approximately two hours before her body was found; death at five A.M. The statement given for the cause of death revealed Jasmine had been strangled. A televised interview with the man who discovered Jasmine's body, said when he opened the suitcase he saw a small hand but said nothing about body damage. Oddly, four days later the police department issued a different statement claiming disfigurement, a horrifying detail the man did not mention the first time, why? Within two weeks a second Coroner's report was issued changing the time of death and details that opposed the initial Coroner's report in order to match the story detectives pieced together.

They did not address why it took twelve days to discover Jasmine's car a short distance away from home.

Ryan and Jasmine checked into the L'Auberge Hotel on August thirteen at six thirty P.M to attend a poker game hosted for the purpose of fundraising for charity.

Surveillance showed Ryan and Jasmine leaving the Hilton where the function was held at two thirty A.M. on August fourteen. That same morning surveillance shows Ryan leaving the L'Auberge Hotel at nine A.M.

The camera does not show the private patio entrance to their suite on the main floor where Jasmine could walk out into the parking lot undetected and get in the car. With most couples the man carries out the luggage and checks out at the front desk.

Detectives reported Jasmines death took place in the Hotel August fourteen but initially the coroner reported her death occurred two hours before her body was found the morning of August fifteen.

The dates and times of surveillance videos do not jive with detective reports which were in conflict with the coroner's initial findings.

Ryan reported to the police that on their return to L.A. on the evening of August fourteen, Jasmine dropped him off at the apartment, and then left to do some errands. Jasmine's Mercedes was eventually found in a parking lot in West Hollywood one mile from their apartment. When Jasmine left Ryan to do her errands could she have been attacked in the bank parking lot as she was returning to her car with cash in hand? Was this crime a robbery to steal her cash and Mercedes that went terribly wrong? Were Jasmine's body disposed of and her car stolen as part of an organized crime ring whose theft was foiled?

Were they forced to return the car twelve days later because of media and police attention? Police reports provided a perfect opportunity for hiding their crime as eyes turned toward Ryan.

It was not unusual for Jasmine to disappear. Waiting twenty four hours, Ryan phoned the police to report her missing after calling her Mom and friends to see if they had heard from her. Jasmine stayed in contact with friends and during past episodes of disappearing someone always knew her whereabouts.

Reports never fully revealed Jasmine's continued associations with her former husband.

From the beginning it was puzzling why detectives dismissed him as a suspect with little investigation. They were married for a short time having a fiery and turbulent relationship and it was Jasmine who instigated proceedings for a divorce. Police discovered love letters he saved from Jasmine and love letters he had written to Jasmine during his time in prison.

The letters indicated they were still involved even physically while he was there. His mother was quoted saying "their relationship was very volatile at times." While married it was reported they were involved with buying and selling illegal drugs.

I have had a million "what ifs" running through my mind and would be remiss if I did not pose the one over whelming question, so I ask, what if he had a motive assuming mistakes made by Jasmine resulted in the charges that sent him to prison? He was convicted because Jasmine made a deal with the police to walk free. She kept their money and secured her freedom by presenting evidence against him. Jasmine continued to let him feel there was hope for reconciliation once he was released by visiting and writing to him during his term. When the day arrived for his release from prison, Jasmine was very nervous of what his intentions would be and whether he still carried a grudge against her.

She arranged the two day reunion, accompanied by family members, to take place at a beach feeling protected by public eyes and family while she assessed his feelings.

The scene was portrayed as a celebration of his freedom as Jasmine warmly pressed a pose of closeness.

He was cool but accommodating, allowing her to relax in the façade of friendship. Jasmine's wedding band was absent from her finger as she had not yet told him she had remarried, preferring to break the news face to face to assess his reaction.

Listening to the assaulting news and willing his virile temper into control, his mind set itself into Sicilian law, and raged in lethal anger.

As they parted with amiable promises of seeing each other soon, did he seal his intention following tradition with a final "kiss of death?" Was he overcome by jealousy and betrayal once he knew the truth of her marriage to Ryan?

Did his anger overcome him once he discovered the depth of Jasmine's deception leading to his conviction? What if he orchestrated the perfect plan of murder, creating an alibi for himself, part of a lurid evil plan as an unknown person lured Jasmine to her death. Police initially remarked "it seems a professional hit" due to the lack of forensic evidence needed to build a case.

Strangely coincidental and somewhat convenient that after his release from prison on August eleven, her former husband was arrested for a parole violation the same day Jasmine's body was found on August fifteen, not forgetting that two out of five of those days had been spent with Jasmine. He also lived in San Diego, not far from the poker game that Ryan and Jasmine attended the last night they were seen together. Was his arrest on purpose removing him from immediate access and questioning by the media? From what I read, he had a record of assault along with drug charges that put him behind bars.

From the beginning detectives remarked Jasmines murder seemed to be professional, a sentiment that many have shared. Crime scenes never left any trace of evidence for police to convict any one person.

It remains an unsolved case.

It is believed Jasmine did have ties to organized crime. When word circulated she "wanted out" too many powerful names were at risk of disclosure and Jasmine had witnessed too much; she was a money making commodity for others who would not let her go.

Ryan became an unknowing patsy and a perfect storm was set into motion; a phone call and text message from a previous lover; Ryan's reaction triggering Jasmines temper providing the visible alibi needed to keep attention on Ryan.

On the afternoon they returned to L.A. Jasmine told Ryan she was going out to do some shopping but did not return from her errands that evening. Had Jasmine agreed to meet the man she spoke with the previous night?

The next morning Ryan called his Mom telling her of the latest troubles with Jasmine and that she had run away again. His Mom, upset, suggested he come home right away. He needed to leave in a couple of days for his visa hearing in Canada anyway, so agreed he would.

After waiting two days to hear from Jasmine, he packed for his trip, drove to Las Vegas to get his boat knowing it may take time before his new green card would be issued, called police from Utah telling them where he was headed, and was unaware of the brewing media frenzy as he slowly drove north.

Detectives said there had been a struggle during Jasmine's attack; she had long nails, perhaps she had bitten her assailant and forensic evidence could have linked her killer from skin under the nails or teeth marks. Ryan's body had no scratches or bite marks or bruises of any kind. During one interview a police investigator said they were looking for a second person. I had an intuitive impression it may have been two possibly three people that murdered Jasmine.

I also felt the crime took place in a public space, even where children would have played.

In a dream Ryan showed me a picture of himself in what looked like a soccer or rugby uniform and at first it never made any sense. Months later I now believe he was trying to point to a sports field next to a park.

Since childhood Ryan fainted each time he had blood tests, or at the sight of blood whether on himself or others.

Last summer he received a piece of barbequed chicken with blood in the center and became nauseated and pale almost throwing up. He literally became physically ill at the sight of blood and would have been incapable of inflicting the injuries he was accused of.

No matter what we tried to say, or do Ryan was considered guilty long before evidence was gathered. Police did not have to spend taxpayers' money on expensive forensics when the media carried out their investigation and delivered a conviction on their behalf. I was perplexed, along with many people, to understand the obvious biased condemnation from the Orange County District Attorney's office which quickly led investigations solely towards Ryan.

It is possible the discovery of Jasmine's body was not by chance, that instructions were given to the time and place eliminating the risk of her body disappearing.

This act may have been part of instilling fear and control in others with ideas of leaving the business. Jasmine may have unwittingly raised red flags to the wrong people when she announced her intentions and desires for a new life. If so, her body had to be found quickly to carry out the message to others.

Strangely, Jasmine's unique Mercedes who authorities and general public were asked to search for took twelve days to discover only blocks away from their condo in a public parking lot near a bank and shops.

Of course when found it was parked away from the angle of surveillance cameras and curiously video coverage is missing showing only certain images and time frames or none at all where it should have in key locations.

Suspiciously it was "friends of Jasmine" who finally told police where the car was located.

So many people have agreed from the very beginning this is a story of organized crime. Yet here we are in Canada so far away; no one wanting to hear what we knew about Ryan's life or circumstances around the death of two young people who were caught in a web of deception, lies, and evil.

Not even police or detectives made contact to ask what we may have known.

Two families have suffered an incredible loss of young lives that were just taking roots.

I am patient and believe those who are responsible will create their own demise, and in the future will not be able to go to their grave without releasing their burden.

One day someone will speak the truth.

Our truth is we have lost our Ryan until we meet again in spirit.

We are so grief stricken and heartbroken it will imprint our souls for a thousand lifetimes.

Life will never feel the same, even on a happy day for a brief moment I can feel a heartbeat of sadness and loss before I remind myself I must accept it.

It is unnatural for parents to bury their children. Dan will never be the same man; he is broken. There are no words powerful enough to describe the pain I have seen in my brother. I will be haunted by these visions and feelings for the rest of my days.

My memories of Dan holding his baby son, knowing the love and joy that filled his heart, burn so deeply in loss and sorrow.

Dan was a doting, nurturing, loving, supportive father who provided opportunities for his son to develop his interests in life. They had a loving, enviable father and son relationship; they were best friends.

Ryan is gone from our lives and we will cherish the precious thirty two years we shared with him.

The night Ryan died I awoke at three fifteen in the morning hearing his voice calling my name. He said "Linda pay attention, his hands were cupping my face and looking intently into my eyes, listen to me. You must tell Dad to get my computer. There is something he needs to have." I began sobbing with unbearable pain and asking him why? Why? He said the moment he died he felt such relief to be away from the pain and horrifying experience. By trying to get Jasmine away events were set in motion that no one could have stopped.

He told me to rest, that he would come again. I said nothing to anyone, wondering about my own state of mind and delusions.

Two nights later I awoke again at three fifteen A.M. and Ryan was there. I saw his face as clearly as in life. We began a conversation of questions and answers as he explained in vivid description how lives are always about learning from our experiences allowing souls to grow towards greater enlightenment and wisdom in the human journey.

This is what he said and showed me. Sometimes a soul will choose an extremely hard experience as part of their soul's evolution.

Ryan showed me thousands of people affected by this dramatic tragic event he and Jasmine orchestrated.

They did not knowingly on a human level create it, rather agreed to be a part even before they were born.

Souls have a predestined pathway from choices made in spirit form before we are born into physical form.

I saw fathers' hearts soften towards their sons offering better guidance in relationships, mothers, who by making one decision altered the futures of their daughters keeping them safe, young men and women seeing clearly the dangers in their own relationships changing the course of their lives.

I saw expressions of grief, anger, sadness, despair, tears, judgment, prayers, hope, sorrow, and horror, panic, disbelief, and anguish in people around the world who had been affected by this tragedy.

I saw through Ryan and Jasmine's sacrifice many souls learned lessons they too needed for growth in the journey of life.

This horrible experience had touched, changed and saved many lives in ways we would not know of on this side.

When the media began to disappear Ryan's memorial was planned. It would be private and by invitation only to eliminate the prying eyes of the world.

Miracle

Our world and reality during the past month was blurry, teetering on the brink of collapse and insanity.

On September twenty John fell into a state of grief wanting to numb his emotional pain with alcohol, drinking into unconsciousness from morning to night.

On the afternoon I accompanied my brother and mother to the cemetery, John bought his last bottle consuming its contents between five and eleven o'clock.

The next morning I heard a thump in the other room and got up to see what happened. John was still intoxicated but said he thought he had fallen. I asked if he was okay and he said he thought so and was going back to bed.

It was four days from Ryan's memorial; we were preparing to say our final farewells. I went about my day periodically checking on John passed out like the previous five days. When I checked him at noon I noticed he had not moved and thought by now he should have started to sober. He barely responded when I talked to him.

Normally I would have sensed danger sooner but was in a state of exhaustion and emotional impairment from the extreme conditions we had lived through the past month. I was uncertain if John had sustained an injury when he fell or if alcohol had poisoned his body. When the ambulance arrived John was not responsive and the paramedics began speaking of stroke or brain injury as he was rushed into the trauma ward for emergency surgery. The neurosurgeon said John's pupils were already dilated and he did not think his chances of surviving surgery were probable.

He had a subdural hematoma and the pressure from the ruptured blood vessel had compressed his brain. I looked deeply into the surgeon's eyes and said this man has a brilliant mind, he must live.

Oh God, how could this be happening? That night I fell into dark hours of indescribable pain, fear, and anguish.

I could barely breathe fighting to control the shaking and wails that seemed unearthly. A social worker asked if there was family to contact for saying their goodbyes. No one thought John was going to live.

As family arrived we barely spoke as we each relived our own memories with John as he lay in the operating room fighting to live.

Many hours later the surgeon came out to say they removed two blood clots and cauterized the broken blood vessel in his brain. He estimated that when John came to emergency he was one hour away from death as his pupils were already "blown out." The surgeon said there was nothing else they could do for John and now we had to wait and see.

He was moved into the intensive care unit, I was given a beeper and told to go home and get some rest.

When I returned to the hospital John was on full life support with tubes in and out of everywhere and looked awful but by the grace of God was still with us. He had endured a major seizure during the night; common after brain surgery but was stable.

While visiting, one of the doctors came by and said not to get my hopes up because it was such a severe injury he might not make it. I crumbled into heaving sobs of uncertainty until the I.C.U. nurse observing John throughout the night said aside from the seizure John was stable and peaceful and that was a positive sign.

I returned home that night feeling devastated with grief, the unfairness of life, and helpless. After a while calmness came over me and I knew what I had to do. I lay down and began the deep breathing of preparing, clearing and connecting to universal life energy. I prayed until I saw the familiar face of Jesus that was present in all healing sessions. My prayer was demanding with a spark of anger that I would not accept anything less than a complete total healing for John.

95

I visualized my hands on John's head as he lay in the hospital and prayed for the healing energy of Jesus to come through me into John.

As my hands lay on his head, I begged for a miracle for him to be completely healed. My hands glowed with intense white energy light and they became so hot they burned. I sat in complete focus and intention of love and healing for John for a very long time.

Eventually I let go and sat back in a state of peace. I drifted off into sleep feeling John was going to be okay.

As news spread to his family John's Sister Janis, living in Edmonton, decided to read her oracle cards by Doreen Virtue and the following three cards fell into her lap.

The first card was Miracle Healing and it read expect a miracle. You have prayed for assistance, and it is forthcoming. The more completely you surrender your situation to God, the more rapidly you will realize your healing.

The second card was Detoxification and it read you are being guided to clean your body, environment, mind and heart of toxins. God will help you with this endeavor.

The third card was Breaking Free and it read do you feel trapped in some life area? This card asks you to take the first step in freeing yourself from any unnatural restrictions.

For the next five days John went into alcohol and nicotine withdrawals. He had to be tied down and restrained from injuring himself and pulling out tubes.

He mumbled and moaned twisting his body and at times tried to open his eyes to see around him but the effort was exhausting.

Those were very anxious days but I was sure he responded as I stroked and kissed his cheeks telling him how much I loved him and that we were not finished with our lives together.

It was a thrilling moment when they removed his breathing apparatus on day seven as John was taken out of the intensive care unit and moved to the neurological unit for his recovery.

Throughout the week prayer chains were sent across the country for John by friends and family, sending hundreds of powerful prayers up to the heavens. The next few days were amazing as John began moving forward quickly with his recovery. He started to recognize and whisper our names and although he was easily confused and tired quickly we began to be hopeful the John we all loved so dearly was still there.

Out of the blue he asked, "Who hit me over the head?" and then weakly tried to laugh. I was over the moon with happiness as not only was he speaking in a full sentence but the emotion of humor was there as well.

Next he wanted his glasses and when they removed his feeding tube and catheter he relished real food and willingly accepted help going to the bathroom.

On day twelve I cut his toe nails and fingernails, and his lopsided hair to match his shaved left side.

I helped him into a shower where he sat while we washed his head and body.

Just three days ago the social worker spoke of wheelchair and full time caregiving, telling me to prepare myself for a different life.

The head nurse said she had been on this ward for twenty five years and with the severity of John's injury claimed no one recovered one hundred per cent and that he would never fully recover enough to return to his job.

Two neurosurgeons came in on day ten and gave the same verdict.

Everywhere I turned I received the worst despairing news; no one was willing to give any hope. It was an emotional roller coaster of heart pounding joy and heart wrenching sadness full of uncertainty each and every day.

John's progress was phenomenal and by day sixteen even the doctors and nurses began to agree they were surprised. It was decided he was ready to move to the rehabilitation ward, and we were told that a normal stay in rehab was four months as the brain would need stimulation in all areas. We settled in for the months ahead; each day scheduled with several types of therapies that would help John regain his physical strength and co-ordination as well as mental and social skills.

John was given day passes on weekends and was soon allowed to spend weekend nights at home, which thrilled me but created anxiety for John who worried about being away from the safety and care of the hospital.

Our family enjoyed a wonderful Thanksgiving dinner as we sat with deepest gratitude looking at John's smiling face eating turkey dinner.

Test after test proved John had not lost any brain function, even the complicated electrical engineering and technical design skill was still present and functioning.

Finally after eight weeks in the hospital John was released and allowed to come home, a whopping two full months ahead of schedule that John's medical caregivers had anticipated. I felt ecstatic, grateful, and overcome with repressed emotion from the traumatic past three months of our lives.

John and I fell into the busy schedule of doctor's appointments, rehab therapies, and reorganizing our lives that had been on hold for months. His recovery has been remarked as "a miracle" by medical staff on all levels. Each and every day I witness a beautiful miracle unfolding right before my eyes. There are some recoveries that doctors simply cannot explain; it just happens.

Our joy was soon clouded by sadness as John's mother began to lose her long battle with cancer. She was firm in her decision to remain at home and her three daughters became living angels meeting their mother's wishes.

Christmas came, John had been home for one month and our hearts were again tempered with happiness and sorrow. It was immensely difficult celebrating the birth of Jesus as our hearts were so heavy with the absence of Ryan and the illness of John's mother.

We celebrate Christmas day with John's family and on our arrival John's mother greeted us wearing her Mrs. Santa hat looking adorable and as always full of loving spirit. She wanted this last Christmas with her family and even managed to sit at the dinner table and give us a Christmas blessing. The next twenty days of her life were spent in preparation for leaving her worldly life and joining her heavenly father and family.

On the night of her passing we gathered to share dinner with brother and sisters as they reassured their mother she was surrounded by her children.

I sat beside her bed and prayed placing my hands on her body sending love and peace. As I placed my hand on her crown chakra and solar plexus I realized her soul was in the process of leaving the body and knew I should not interfere.

Janis asked what I thought and I said I felt their mother was leaving tonight.

I gently suggested John say what he needed for the last time and looking down at this lovely woman knew she was a powerful force joining the loving oneness of God.

I was struck with emotion feeling the full force of wonderment in the miracle of birth and the miracle of death. She left this world two hours later with her daughters by her side.

Never Grow Old

The day came that John moved out of the home which meant hiring day and night time caregivers. Mom's confusion was unmanageable and her broken heart inconsolable with his absence. At times her anguish was too much for her to bear resulting in behavior that could turn violent putting the safety of others and her at risk. Within months there were no longer blinds on windows and curtains had been shredded from her erratic storms of frustration. During episodes of venting her anger anything within reach was hurled in all directions along with shocking verbal profanities, seemingly possessed. Mom was hurt and angry facing her greatest fear of John leaving once again, but this time dementia robbed her of functionally processing emotions, leaving her raw and primal.

After living on his own for six months John realized that moving back into the home where he too could be cared for was a better alternative, even though it meant witnessing Mom's dysfunction every day. Mom was soothed having him home but battles over suspicions of women in the home dominated daily life. Her wailing frustrations were relentless and exhausting leaving us to feel drained and stunned.

Geriatric specialists could offer few suggestions other than antipsychotics which in the end worsened hysteria and deepened psychosis. John's mental health began to show decline as he couldn't deal with Mom's advancing personality deterioration and began depending more on family and the live in caregiver for his needs alongside of Mom. He and the caregiver developed camaraderie acting as sounding boards for each other's problems and offered mutual emotional support on difficult days. I will refer to her simply as "B". This woman was very dramatic and fiery tempered but spunky and energetic when caring for Mom and on the outside things looked okay. B would fuss with Moms clothes, hair and makeup, sing and jovially go about the day preparing meals and watching over Mom's needs. On days when John annoyed her I listened, soothed, and advised, sometimes for hours until she calmed enough to return home. Her complaints were endless, tiring and always revolved around money but I felt obligated to keep the peace, so relied on my inner dialogue to maintain a calm demeanor while physically tense and irritated. To describe how her personality affected me can be likened to fingernails rasping across a black board. She did many things that gave legitimate reasons for terminating her employment but John begged me not to let her go and insisted she was good to Mom so I relented solely for that reason. I was getting ready for work when a frantic call came from John that Mom had collapsed and was lying on the floor unconscious. I could hear B in the background wailing as I asked what happened and how long had she been unconscious? He asked for me to come immediately as he thought she was dying and I said call 911. When I arrived paramedics were standing over Mom who lay in a fetal position on the floor for forty minutes. I looked into their eyes which confirmed everyone's suspicion that Mom was passing away. I lay down on the floor beside Mom holding her close while kissing her gently and whispering loving words. I willed a cocoon of energy around both of us infusing her body with heat and visualizing silver and golden energy swirling in our egg shaped bubble. Suddenly she jolted and with fear in her voice cried out "Linda, where was I? I don't want to be there, help me." She was panicked and breathing rapidly until I soothed her the best way I knew how. The paramedics stepped in and prepared to take her to the hospital but I felt reluctant to let go until they assured me they would take good care of my Mother. No definitive medical answer was found of what happened that morning. One Doctor surmised it may have been a seizure, paramedics were awed by what they witnessed and I felt Mom was probably on her passing journey but feeling familiar energy, was drawn back. That afternoon she was released from the hospital totally healthy and revitalized.

On one of my days to care for Mom my attention was drawn to a document on the coffee table and since I looked after financing and bill payments thought it was left for me. It was a bill of sale signed by John as the purchaser for a brand new Mercedes Benz. I was stunned, how could he afford to buy a new car?

A month later B drove up in her new Mercedes and I could not hold back my questions of how and where did the money come from. I was left with an unsatisfactory answer from both B and John who basically said it was none of my business which left me to ponder and fume in thoughts of suspicion and conspiracy.

The following summer B started a new campaign to get John out of the home. She began telling stories of John abusing Mom mentally when her failing eyesight made bathroom visits more challenging. He yelled and cursed throwing fits and tantrums banging his head on walls and throwing his body on the floor as onlookers considered him a madman. Visiting nurses listened to B's stories in earnest and witnessed John's agitated mental state determining he should be removed from the home.

Here we are one year later poor Mother is hysterical as once again John leaves her and horrifying chaos pursues. Further into dementia there was nothing we could do this time to soothe her anguished mind and in desperation turned to drugs to sedate her from harming herself. These were dark days seeing Mother's will to live fading right before our eyes because of one person. More people were hired for night shifts and another full time person for days but B was perturbed that I would not let her take full responsibility. For the month of July I consented but my intuition kept nagging that something was not right. I began dropping in unannounced which really ruffled her feathers and further raised my suspicions. One evening a neighbor questioned where John was and who was taking care of the house? He said there were strange things going on and loud parties which gave him concerns for Dyma's welfare. It became clear that B had campaigned to remove John from the home so she could live in the house alone to entertain her friends with no interference. It took only two days before I hired more caregivers and limited her shifts.

Bizarre things began to happen to Mom, the house and night staff and B kept saying she did not trust these new people alone with Mom. She insisted on returning to the house on her days off and spending the night to keep an eye on things because in her words, "I am dedicated to your Mom". On one visit I noticed Mom's hand was blue and bruised and B blamed it on a new girl, another visit Mom had a long nasty bruise on her spine and again B blamed the girl. No one would admit to what happened and my panic deepened in fears of my poor mother suffering abuse at the hands of strangers. I had to let the new person go and believe the story B gave.

Damage continued within the home and the stories were always the same, Mom had a behavioral meltdown, and B needed more money to deal with the difficulty. I received calls at all hours of the day and night from B dramatizing events, claiming Mom's disease was unmanageable and requesting to sedate her more often for control. By now I was aware of her antics and alligator tears as ploys for more money and instead responded by saying things like "well B, maybe you have reached a time that we should cut back your hours or maybe this job has become too much for you to handle;" then immediately she would change her tone of voice assuring me Mom had settled down.

I held firm to the decision of no drugs during the day which had been a constant battle with John and B wanting to sedate Mom day and night. During the past year many times I would arrive to take Mom out for lunch and an afternoon of shopping only to find her slumped over with her head on her stomach and drool oozing from the corners of her mouth; totally incoherent, due to their insistence on drugging her to keep her calm for peace and quiet.

I arrived one summer morning finding mother half naked and crouched against a tree and ran to her asking what happened. Mom desperately clung to me saying this woman is crazy, protect me, and don't leave me alone with her. B said she had let Mom wander outside to calm down because Mom was unmanageable.

Now here is where it gets crazy in your own head because yes, dementia can cause uncooperative behavior but clearly Mom was frightened, so who do you believe?

B blamed accidents in the home on other people claiming they were incompetent and lazy, refusing to accept responsibility for any mishaps herself. Tensions in the home rose to a feverous pitch leaving me to umpire the posturing roosters circling each other waiting to strike.

Without any known reason Mom began having recurring nosebleeds leaving spilled blood on the white bedroom carpet, walls, duvet cover, sheets, pillows and bathroom floor. The caregiver working the night shift stopped the bleeding but left Mom to sleep in bloodied pajamas and bed linens. It took five hours to clean up the blood and three hundred dollars to steam clean the carpets. I was upset, venting frustrations because mother was left with caked blood on her body and left to walk through pooled blood to get to the bathroom. A few nights later a tap in the sink was turned on flooding the bathroom and bedroom and a few days later diarrhea spattered the freshly cleaned carpet.

B had previously claimed Mom needed depends because she was showing signs of incontinence which I questioned wholeheartedly as never before had Mom not made it to the toilet. I discovered B was using them for her own bladder incontinence. A few days later I received a phone call from B on Friday morning declaring Mom would need more depends because her stomach was upset and would probably have diarrhea in the afternoon. B's shift ended at noon. I drove out to see if Mom was ill and at the time she was fine but just in case I left a few depends instead of a whole box. The next afternoon two of the caregivers asked to meet with me at the house. I drove out immediately as they sounded very upset and they took me into the bathroom to show me some fluorescent yellow stains on the toilet, tile grout and one of the diapers. They were scared of what was coming out of Mom as she was very sick and weak but also because the stains could not be removed and appeared more chemical like. They said they had worked in care homes and had seen a lot of diarrhea but nothing like this and began revealing stories of B's past treachery.

The previous accidents were of B's doing, she had mixed some ingredients to look like diarrhea and spread it on the carpet to make the caregiver on shift look negligent. She had snuck in during the night while another caregiver was sleeping and turned on the tap which caused the flood.

The past summer B had purposefully bruised Moms hand, kicked her in the leg and let her fall backwards into the tub bruising her spine in efforts to get the other caregivers dismissed. As people discovered her treachery they quietly left instead of telling me of the abuse because they were threatened by B and afraid of her wrath. B wanted everyone to look incompetent and have me think she was the only one with enough experience to care for Dyma in order to restore her dominance over the home. I discovered B had been evicted from her daughter's home months ago due to her horrific gambling addiction which clarified her desperate need for a place to live. She lived rent free in our home for months as well as receiving a handsome salary but complained bitterly for more money.

Following Moms weird diarrhea incident the week was spent nursing her back to health but the next Friday as B left at noon Mom began getting very sick again in the afternoon, evening and all day Saturday and Sunday.

We began frantic efforts to help her failing health but when B came back from her weekend off Mom began to refuse food or drink. She would spit anything that was placed near her mouth clamping her lips tight.

For the next three days no one could get even an eye dropper of fluid in her mouth and she drifted away into a state of sleep and dehydration. I phoned paramedics because I did not think she would make it through the night without fluids and admitted her to the hospital. It took another twelve hours before doctors examined her and with a lot of vexation and coaxing on my part they agreed to give her intravenous fluids. It only took a couple of hours for Mom to become responsive and lucid.

After another twelve hours of fluids the doctors said they were sending her home. What? No tests? By the admission of medical staff my mother almost died and they were not going to investigate why? We were told that because Mom was ninety one they could not justify the costs for medical staff to care for her in I.C.U. Also because there was no definitive illness, accident or medical condition they saw no reason to admit her to hospital even though we begged them to give her a little more time with I.V fluids. The truth behind their words was that it is time to let your mother die because she is old. Mom came home from the hospital feeling well for the first twenty four hours and even drank small amounts of fluid but after B's shift she was back to refusing food or drink. That night I had a very lucid dream where I walked back in time watching events with B and Mom during the past three weeks. I saw how B was forcing this horrible stuff in Moms mouth and Mom desperately fighting her off. The look of malice on B's face was the devil incarnated as she yelled and cursed even shoving and holding Mom down while she poured this foul, poisonous fluid down her throat.

It all began to make perfect sense once the events were in order until I knew beyond any doubt in my entire being that B was poisoning Mom.

I flew out of bed, rushed out to the house and peered in through the window to see B jamming a spoon in Moms mouth. I yelled to get her attention running inside as B quickly dumped the drink and said she was trying to spoon feed juice as Mom was still refusing to drink. My whole body vibrated from coursing emotions yet I knew the importance of stilling my mind long enough for logical thinking to discover what I knew to be true. I shadowed B's every move never leaving Mom alone in her weakened semi-conscious state, even climbing in bed with her to keep her warm and allowing no one to touch or feed her. Knowing we were losing precious time I ventured cautiously with immense concern in my voice and asked B the question; is there anything unusual that you have fed Mom which may cause adverse reactions as it is odd that after your shift Mom becomes very sick.

She looked at me oddly until I said; well I have to find the cause of Mom's sickness so I am ordering a toxicology test today. B jumped up and did not even try to defend herself even though I had not outright accused her, and flew into the closet to pack her things. She was frantic and wide eyed the usual over confident bravado subdued by obvious fear. There was no protest when I told her she was fired; she was gone within five minutes.

Mom began failing quickly and I desperately called homecare who turned the case over to the palliative team because they did not think we would make it through the next forty eight hours. We begged them to rehydrate her with intravenous fluids and this time it was done in the home. The whole family gathered to say farewells as truly Mom was in the throes of death. She was approaching two weeks of no food and eyedroppers of liquid we managed to squeeze in her mouth. It was days before Christmas and carefully the palliative nurse asked if we wanted Mom to pass at home or be transferred to a hospice. My heart quietly filled with grief.

I remember this moment as a beautiful sunny morning with hoarfrost heavily laden on branches when one of our caregivers, believing in its healing properties, brought a generator quartz crystal to place around Moms neck. It was like a pinch to awaken me as I had been so wrapped in feelings of grief and sadness that all was forgotten of healing from a higher power. I felt a deep sense of gratitude and began praying and working energetically to clear Mom's field.

I used a crystal on each center to absorb and clear stagnant energy and to create movement in the chakras while the caregiver continued praying. While in a deep trance-like state I visualized her body healing and re-charging from our energetic connection when suddenly her eyes flew open and Mom asked for a cup of coffee. Startled that she spoke and doubly startled she wanted to drink after two weeks of no food or fluid I could only think of the word miracle. The caregiver and I could hardly believe what we witnessed. Although she was very weak we managed to sit her at the table to drink her coffee and then she asked for a cookie!

It was Christmas Eve morning and I was to prepare turkey dinner following the Scandinavian tradition. Family was coming to perhaps spend our last Christmas with our mother, grandmother, great-grandmother, sister, aunt and wife. Dyma had many roles with the family that came to adore and love her this evening.

109

Sitting around the dinner table surrounded by tradition and love, Kimberlee desired to feed her grandmother and with full shock and gaping mouths we all put down our forks and watched in amazement as Mom ate a complete and hardy meal. Next she joined in to sing Christmas carols, although weakly, she sang. Do you think we were ever given a more wonderful Christmas gift in our lives?

For the next six weeks Dyma's healing was phenomenal, becoming stronger each day both physically and mentally. The one thing that did not stop was the horrific nosebleeds that occurred up to five times a day. It could take two people to hold Mom still long enough to compress a cold cloth or put pressure on her nose, combat and fear overtaking her mind that we were harming her. I am traumatized in memory of three women slipping on the bathroom floor in pools of blood gushing from Mom's nose and mouth holding not cloths but towels soaked in blood amidst screams and flailing arms.

Choking and vomiting sprays of blood left the walls and floors to look like a crime scene from CSI. Paramedics were called a few times but they offered no advice and left once they knew the bleed was under control.

New humidifiers were installed on the furnaces and a portable one added to her bedroom to improve air quality. We administered high doses of cod liver oil and vitamin D to heal the delicate tissues internally and topically applied herbal salve in her nostrils and everything worked well until in a drowsy state her finger found its way to remove the annoying clot and blood flowed again. Saline nose sprays, lubricants, nothing could stop the morning bleeds for four months. Finally she allowed gloves to stay on her hands, only because they felt warm; feeling cold was her constant nemesis. Slowly the bleeding subsided.

The day B left I searched and found a jar of foul smelling dark brown rotten fish labeled **Do Not Eat** in the fridge with a fluorescent yellow substance settled on the bottom.

I hid it in the garage to deal with later however my husband inadvertently threw it away. Camera images were out of focus and inconclusive so without the evidence to prove abuse we were left with no hope of pursuing justice.

We were advised that what we saw her doing even with witness corroboration would not hold up in court. I am convinced that anti-freeze was mixed with rotten fish.

Further investigations into her past led to truths that revealed a deceitful sociopathic personality.

Two other persons had fallen sick from an unknown substance hidden in their food. She had been charged with negligence causing death of an elderly man in her care at a nursing home she previously worked.

Several years ago she left her husband and three young daughters for a man in California whom she resided with for many years while honing her con artist skills.

B befriended recent immigrants who paid her large sums of money to get a loved one into the country sooner, leading them to believe she had connections to speed up the immigration process. When word of her scam travelled through the community people banded together to charge her with fraud which sent her to jail. Her jail sentence led to deportation to Canada, barring her entrance into the U.S permanently.

Part of her con was to present false papers claiming she was part of the Marcos dynasty stating she would inherit millions once the estate was settled and that some monies were being held in a Swiss bank account until legal processes took its course. The unsuspecting victim was flashed a stamped government seal document while B sweetly talked her way into a "loan" promising to repay once the funds were released.

Unbelievable yet true some people gave her fifty, twenty, ten, or five thousand dollars with no security or promissory note. B frequented casinos which was her social network and place of debauchery.

Finally after word spread of her unpaid debts twelve people brought fraud charges against her resulting in another jail sentence in Canada. The evidence kept mounting in shocking numbers of cases where people had been financially destroyed by deceitful practices from this woman. In fact it seemed she had made a career of preying on the vulnerabilities of innocent and elderly citizens.

After B was fired she continued to drive the Mercedes that John had co-signed, registered and insured. She had defaulted on several payments during the past year and wrote fraudulent reimbursements to John who had to cover her monthly payments.

He finally admitted the financial arrangement regarding the car and the fact that B promised to look after him financially for the rest of his life once she received her inheritance. That promise hit his vulnerable bull's eye. He truly believed her story and that he would never again have to worry about money.

She avoided John's phone calls and true to past performance with no intentions to make car payments, dumped the whole financial burden in John's lap. Police advised John to take legal action immediately or just take back his car.

After many failed attempts he finally found the car parked outside a casino, drove his own car out of site and walked up to the Mercedes and drove away.

When B came outside to find the car missing she became hysterical screaming for security to help.

Once they discovered the details that in reality it was not her car they left her standing all alone with nothing.

Her former husband evicted B from his property and all her worldly possessions were in the car which she had been living in, a sad testament to gambling addiction. Although John retrieved the Mercedes he did not recover any of the twenty five thousand loaned to B nor did his sister, also a victim, who had loaned her six thousand. The list of unpaid debts to other people is long and heartbreaking knowing they will never see their hard earned money returned.

The lesson learned about hiring a caregiver is; do not always trust recommendations and background histories given by agencies get an independent security check on a person's history through police. Be vigilant and involved in your loved ones care. The saying is so true, "when the cat is away, the mice will play." Look for the smallest clue your loved one may give that all is not right and trust your instinct; after all, you know them better than anyone.

After living through the six month nightmare we made the decision to have Mom live with us to oversee her care. We lost all privacy and freedom in daily life as full time caregivers were in our home twenty four/seven. Admittedly the choice added stress and never ending involvement in the exhausting and emotionally draining disease of dementia. There was no escape within the home from the background chaos and constant mishaps. We became caregivers of the caregivers.

In Alberta a new rule came into effect that if you placed your loved one on the waiting list for transition services to find a long term care facility you had to accept the first available bed within a radius of one hundred kilometers. This means you and family have no choice where or what happens to your loved one. It is a nerve-racking process and many facilities are so crowded it reminds one of suffering puppies in "puppy mills" left helpless in deplorable conditions. A bed placed in an eight foot by five foot room space, a curtain separating another soul and a bathroom shared by four people is the allotted privacy. It seems that prisoners have better living conditions than these poor souls who are at the end of their lives. What has happened to the well-deserved respect and compassion for the fruitful, productive contributions these people have given to society?

Baby boomers will soon be entering those out dated facilities and unless the topic is brought into an open forum to inspire change the pitfalls of despair and tragedy will continue. Overcrowding will become catastrophic with swelling numbers of boomers ill prepared and miserable with what awaits them. The truth is unless we have saved a lot of money for private care it is a doom and gloom ending that awaits most.

Nursing homes has long been an uncomfortable topic, one we hope we never have to experience, and one that is pushed to the back of our minds. This generation still has time to ensure that kinder regard to the size of personal living space will allow comfort and dignity. Some newly built facilities are addressing these issues creating homey environments yet they still continue to house two people to a room.

Many of our elderly citizens are treated as unwanted cast offs of society, drugged into submission for ease of care, left alone in silent beds and wheel chairs throughout our country. The halls of nursing homes are lined with despondent people, heads hanging and helplessly confined at the mercy of others. To commit mother into a facility of this description breaks my heart and yet the time comes that a ravaged brain requires care beyond what home environments can offer. Perhaps we need to take a second look at our quest for living longer. Why would we want to live to be one hundred when quality of life is reduced to an inkling of joy?

As a child I witnessed great grandparents being cared for in their home by family members and friends in the community until their death. My grandmother was moved into a mobile home behind her former house where she lived independently but assisted daily by Dad, sister, brothers, and family until she passed on. Perhaps that is one reason it has been so difficult to let go of mother's care even with professional recommendation but the difference from then and now is many people provided care and I am only one. Through many tears and heart breaking days the time comes to let our loved ones go. My father's words still echo in my ears, "You have to let me go just like I had to let my mother go, we all go through that passage. I have had a good life and done everything I wanted to do. Be happy for me and enjoy your life."

An instinctive feeling not easily shrugged blended with spiritually honoring life, I ponder why young children are given endless patience and forgiveness, accepted as helpless innocents, yet our elderly members not afforded the same. Impatience and frustrations from ineptness are visible reactions. Society glorifies and sanctifies youth yet it is the shortest phase of life.

Wisdom matures at a ripe old age yet tragically, silently fades into obscurity instead of query. The modern practice is to replace old with new even if things are not worn out or broken. Is this behavior an example of our subconscious mind reflecting distaste for worn out humans?

I struggle with placing mother in a long term care facility just as I worried about placing my daughter in day care.

Isn't there an obvious parallel from early life to late life? Is this a human or cultural flaw how values for new life seem more important than old life? A caregiver from the Philippines told me they did not have nursing homes, the elderly were always cared for by family. Maybe we are a product of birth control; no longer having large families means nursing homes for elderly family.

One morning Mom awoke in a deeper state of panic and delirium crying out for help to bring her home. She was inconsolable in her trance of despair hearing no comforting words around her. The only way I could calm her was to spray an essential oil blend in the air for the limbic center of her brain to shift and redirect a mental pathway as she was stuck in panic.

A minute later it began to work and she began to hear and feel that we were with her. I sat with Mom on the couch and held her close to my body while placing a hand alternately on her crown and brow chakra until she calmed enough for me to speak. I spoke in a low calm voice as the thought occurred to me that in dementia we become lost in our mind creating fear and panic and need someone to bring us back into awareness and reality. I spoke about this being just one life of many and that she would come back in a new life to live with John and her loved ones once again. I suggested she may be finished with her present relationship with John and that she must find a place of peace and accept the life she created and choices she made. I suggested she will have to let go of John and her family at some point as that is what we all do when our bodies wear out and we return to spirit. I spoke of letting go of anxiety over things she can no longer change, to enjoy nature, the sun on her face, the part of being human while on earth that we cannot enjoy in spirit.

I reminded her of the messages her sister and mother had given her after they had passed and that she too would have to bring a message to me.

I spoke of being born knowing we would one day leave this world as the natural occurrence of all things even though it brings sadness. In complete calm she listened then squeezed my hand and nodded her head affirmatively. Mom finally lay back in a state of peace and relaxed her body, exhausted.

No matter how many times we explain she has lived in this home for twenty three years it never soothes Mom's anguished mind of searching for home. It brings me to a pondered point after witnessing four aged family members preparing for their passing.

Each one has spoken the same wish, to go home. Where is home? John's father sat up in bed and declared, take me home, I want to go home now, and then fell back as he drew his last breath. John's mother declared she was going home, and then stated I am leaving now as she exhaled her last breath. My father stated he was ready to go home and see his mother. On the day he passed he said she was standing at the foot of his bed. He said he was going home tonight and then corrected himself by saying well maybe early morning. He passed shortly after midnight.

Do we see a familiar place or become aware of our origins of home as we prepare to leave our body? Why do the earthly homes that we have lived in for many years not feel like home any longer? Humans seem to yearn for a place that seems more familiar, is this our heavenly home that we return to in spirit that we begin to reconnect with at the end of life? I keep wondering if dementia confuses Mom in her search for her spiritual home, that she needs assistance through conversation for understanding the difference. I know through probing that she does not believe where she has lived for twenty three years is home, that Tennessee is not part of her search of home, and that Denmark was once her home but not where she wants to return to. I suppose home remains a mystery until we pass through the tunnel of light ourselves as the veil is lifted on our return home.

Loss is one of the absolutes of life; loss tempers gain, a basic principle creating balance. It is late in life where losses out way the gains when independence and power of choice diminish. Eyesight and hearing weaken, body pain increases, loss of appetite occurs, lack of energy and sleeplessness affect the sense of well-being. Certainly losses increase rapidly after age eighty, even though we are wise old owls out living our bodies, physical loss prepares us for the return to spirit. As Mom weakens walking has become difficult and instead of needing conversation she enjoys peace and quiet while she re-visits her memories and choices made during her life. I can tell she is letting go of her exhausting struggle to finish this life lesson with the man she adored realizing he will not return this time. Her requests for physical needs are silent except for warmth and comfort coming from being cuddled and held close. I spend focused moments enjoying her familiar scent, sound of her voice, her warmth, gazing into the depths of those wise blue eyes and wonderment of how her smile can lift my entire spirit. I practice letting her go from my life but I am selfish and stubbornly resist. We were one of the fortunate families who lucked out with a private room in a newly built facility when Mom had to leave her home at age ninety two. She was placed on the dementia care floor along with twenty five residents. It will remain as one of the most emotionally traumatic days for the family. Watching this frail woman reacting in fear and confusion to her new home tore my heart and the guilt I felt was overwhelming. Everything I had previously promised was fractured leaving me to feel miserable and physically ill. My tortured mind kept screaming what are you doing? How can you leave your Mother in a place like this? Did you not promise to care for her until the end? If you leave her here she will surely die. I was inconsolable in grief praying for forgiveness for placing Mother into a nursing home when I knew that had been her biggest fear for the last stage of life. The only thing that snapped me back was a comment made by my doctor, "Are you willing to die for your mother?"

It is true that caregiver burn out is a reality and many times you become so wrapped up in daily chores and dysfunction you no longer see the effects and toll it takes upon you and your family. Year after year decline of dementia intensifies and you add more and more of your energy and time to manage the disease. It is common for people in their sixties to care for aged parents and instead of enjoying the fruit from laboring years bounce into another full time job of caregiving instead of retirement.

You are thrown into an unfamiliar role with no guide to follow for making right or wrong choices.

In order to ease the transition of moving into the care facility we and Mom's private caregivers stayed with her twenty four seven for the first six weeks while Mom and staff became familiar with individual needs and personality. I brought Mom home for three days and three nights the first few weeks as she adjusted to new sounds, foods, surroundings and people. As we slowly increased her stays she needed someone to be with her during the night to find her way to the bathroom otherwise she would be lost. Eventually we decreased private care to twelve hours a day along with earnest attempts to communicate with staff to get involved with Moms care. Basic things like having a shower or bath were not happening and she did not have one on one feeding which meant Mom was not getting enough food and began losing weight.

Due to her thinness she was always cold so we dressed her in three layers of clothing, undershirt, sweater and vest and gave instruction for staff to do the same however time and again I would arrive to witness Mom in anxiety claiming she was freezing only to find she was wearing a thin undershirt. I had to beg them to turn up the temperature in her room as even I was uncomfortably cold and Mom wore her winter coat to keep warm. I bought a goose down comforter to make sure she was warm at night and one day discovered it had been missing for two nights which meant Mom had slept with no blanket for two sleeps. No wonder she was exhausted and agitated during those two days!

Although I had attached a large label stating DO NOT WASH, in fact it was sent to laundry and was ruined but instead of admitting the mistake tried to discard it in the garbage and pretend it was lost. If we had not raised a fuss and searched for the comforter who knows how long Mom would have slept without a blanket.

The number one concern in long term care is safety. No matter how many times we emphasize to staff that Mom has a type of dementia that renders her blind there is no one around to prevent her from being pushed or slapped by other residents if she happens to get in their way when she walks the halls. She has suffered two black eyes and a bruised body top to bottom along with scrapped legs from wheel chairs and lumps on her head from abuse. It is a miracle she has not broken her hip from the many falls resulting from being pushed down by other residents. The answer to our pleas of concern directed to management is they cannot prevent it. After months of observation during visits I am horrified to find such a lack of staff present at any given time. I cannot count how many times I have had to intervene for safety purpose and referee between fighting residents hitting and pushing each other with no staff on the floor to answer my calls for help.

Mom is still continent and requests to go to the bathroom however because there is no staff to hear her calls she is forced to wear a diaper and with extreme distress suffers humiliation from a basic need. I call this mental torture. On several occasions while walking with Mom I hear residents calling for help to the bathroom and see two staff sitting at the end of the hall talking and laughing while ignoring the residents.

The bottom line is money; nursing homes are under staffed and under educated to the needs of dementia patients.

There is an attitude of apathy and lack of care because broken minds cannot speak truths of their anguish and no one will ever know.

Sadly few have advocates for their needs and safety and perish in ungodly circumstance. It is the reason we cannot put our trust and faith in the nursing home to take over the care of Mom. We provide eight to ten hours of private care each day alongside with what little is provided by the facility to bath, dress and feed Mom. We make sure she gets to the toilet when the urge arises, nails are clipped, hair is groomed, teeth are brushed and human touch and conversation is provided. Most of all our presence keeps her safe from harm as long as we are there. We can only pray that she will survive the night unscathed when left alone. Our utmost goal is to provide comfort and safety and bring some quality of life to her daily routine. We accept there is no getting better from her disease and watch helplessly as it ravages her brain and body. We bring Mom home for family dinners and take her out for drives and coffee hoping it alleviates the boredom she often speaks of but no one knows what amount of familiar stimulus gets through her brain.

It was a normal evening at home as we had just settled to watch TV. I had a wonderful visit with Mom and she was in good spirits when I left in the afternoon. A call from the care center at 9:30 P.M. made my heart race in apprehension. Mom had fallen while walking in the hallway and fell so hard the impact pushed her front teeth right through the skin on her upper lip. I asked the nurse if they were sending her to the hospital but he said he spoke to the Doctor on call by phone and he suggested they treat the injury in the nursing home. In the background I heard Mother sobbing and begging to go home and my heart constricted in painful grief. I grabbed my herbal first aid kit and drove like a mad woman in full rescue mode. On arrival the scene I witnessed will haunt me and I will convulse at the memory until I die. Mom was sobbing, choking on blood, her lip three times its normal size, an open angry gash and the bloody nail clippers, what the hell? An aide was trying to hold ice on her injury; Mom was obviously in a state of shock and all I heard the nurse say was "we have to stop the bleeding." Eyeing the bloodied cloths I asked what the plan of action was and ice was their solution.

121

Then I asked about the bloody nail clippers and was told they had cut the tissue on her lip to free her embedded teeth with NAIL CLIPPERS. I was incredulous to what I heard; taking moments for it to sink in that Mother had literally been tortured cutting fragile tissue with no anesthetic. No wonder she was bleeding profusely and sobbing in pain, her traumatized body shook in convulsion. With a lethal tone of voice I directed them to step away and leave us alone. For the next four hours I used homeopathic remedies to calm her, fresh aloe, arnica and colloidal silver to cleanse the wound, and administered pain killers to ease her discomfort. I placed my hands on the crown and heart chakra alternating hands over her injury and she seemed to know what I was doing as she sat perfectly calm and still, even moving her head toward my hands. The bleeding stopped quickly, her body relaxed and breathing returned to normal. I hydrated her with water and apple juice and cool ice cream helped to numb the brutalized torn tissue inside her mouth. Poor Mother exhausted by trauma felt soothed in the warmth of a daughter's embrace and loving energy. Finally I felt it was safe to let her sleep and tucked her in a cocoon of warm comfort. What we had feared became a reality, she is not safe.

After years of complying with doctors and prescribed pharmaceuticals I finally realized they knew little for treating her rare condition, experimenting with drugs that worsened her condition each time.

Dan and I made the decision to stop drug experimentation after an accidental overdose with Haldolperidol during a hospital stay. The drug caused her to lie with her tongue lolling out the side of her mouth in a comatose state for two and a half days. She was never the same again. They also tied down her hands and restricted her to a chair for so long that when I arrived she was moaning and crying as she sat in a pool of her own waste as no one had paid attention to her plea to use the toilet. This is normal care in hospitals for dementia patients; don't ever kid yourself into believing anything different. We began taking over providing fresh juice we made from vegetables and fruits, homemade nutritional soups and made contact with a clinic in the states with a Neurologist who believed in providing the brain with dense nutrients and supplements needed for optimal functioning. You know there is no cure for dementia but feeding the brain what it needs to be healthy makes perfect sense. I began giving Mom recommended supplements and removed all antipsychotic drugs. Knowing it may take a couple of months to be effective we prepared for agitation and high behavior mood swings as her brain adjusted. It was a miraculous transformation and after a year we knew it had given a quality to her life choosing this route compared to drugged oblivion.

Intercare implemented a new rule that Nurses could only provide medications to residents from Safeway Pharmacy which meant because I ordered and paid for supplements from the states they refused to give them to Mother. The facility offered no alternatives and gave me one hours' notice of ceasing to administer her pills. Luckily private care providers could take over at my request but where are human rights for the helpless when policy deprives families from assisting in the wellbeing of frail elderly loved ones. If we did not have private care to administer the medication needed, Mom would suffer added mental torment due to policy and refusal to administer meds not provided by Safeway. The business decision is favorable only to Safeway and Intercare with no regard of personal needs. Again the attitude of disregarding those that can no longer speak for themselves is deplorable and a reminder we must be advocates for senior citizens. Please always remember you know your loved one better than any medical or care staff.

Although communication is difficult with Alzheimer disease look into their eyes a little deeper, pay attention to their anxiety when they hold a little tighter, try to interpret their emotion or mixed up words and watch body language closely as there are messages being conveyed.

Above all make respectful decisions that have their best interest in your heart and hug them close to you so they still feel loved. Gentle massaging of hands, arms, legs, head and back makes everyone feel good. Human touch is healing and sadly lacking for the elderly. I cut mother's finger and toe nails adding a bowl of warm water to soak in first followed by a hand and foot massage undeniably eliciting immense pleasure. I have taken over cutting, washing and blow drying mother's hair adding a gentle head massage and watch her smile from joyful pampering. I am reminded of administering similar loving care to my infant daughter, life has come full circle. Dementia or Alzheimer's are excruciatingly painful diseases for families to cope with and some simply cannot deal with it.

Current conditions in long term care facilities are disappointing and I suppose the question remains; does anybody care? Is it simply the fate of elderly persons to just fade from life alone and in silence? Advanced dementia is so demanding it requires a team of people to manage care so perhaps the answer is more of coming to terms with our personal limits and accepting what life has brought us, let go of the caregiving role and return to roles of daughter, son, and husband.

A fear resides within that one day my genes may express dementia inherited from maternal family. Alert to new research and always seeking information for preventative practices I include a few suggestions for the sake of interest. Traditional research has focused on ways to remove beta amyloid and tau proteins which have proved to be disappointing.

There seems to be a central key from the latest research pointing to oxidative stress from free radical damage disrupting the control mechanisms of amyloid production that can lead to amyloid build up.

Supplements recommended for preventing oxidative stress are Curcumin, NAcetyl cysteine, Pregnenolone, and pigmented antioxidants such as Astaxanthin. To counter low blood flow to the brain which can cause cerebral atrophy one can take Vinpocetine and fermented Ginseng. The brain needs to have healthy fats such as Omega 3 especially formulated with higher concentrations of DHA. For healthy homeostasis our bodies prefer an alkaline internal environment. Avoiding acid forming foods in excess for example red meat and eating more alkaline forming green foods such as spinach is a healthier choice. Inflammation in the body is a marker to take notice as it seems to be a pre-cursor to many stages of disease including Alzheimer's. In today's world our body is overwhelmed with toxins found in food preservatives, purifying chemicals in water we drink and environmental toxins in air we breathe. The more chemicals we can consciously avoid will undeniably help our metabolic stress and free radical damage to cells.

I for one will consider antioxidants and anti-inflammatory herbal supplements recommended by current research. The latest statistics claim that before age sixty five one in eight people will develop a form of dementia and by age eighty, one in two. Those figures alongside inherited genetics should prompt responsible preventative action.

There is only breath that carries us from the first cry at birth to the last sigh at death.

PART TWO

<u>HEALING</u>

You might say everyone goes through difficulties in life, what's your point? True, there is no one story more significant than another and it is perception that influences reaction or acceptance depending on an individual's history or reference. Dramas occur from those we have relationships with and although a player, we do not always create the illusions but merely react to them through our involvement. In other words if these people had not entered our lives the dramas would not have occurred. So we can say that imprints by associations influence our personality but do not define who we are. We co-create life with others as actors playing a part in each other's play. Every face has a unique story etched in lines that furrow and dimple in expression of fascinating circumstance. Isn't it amazing that from a population of billions we each have unique lives which no two people share identical outcomes due to perception. Just as our DNA is unique so is the blueprint of how we experience life. No one else can chew our food or digest it to sustain life in our body for us just as no one can interpret an emotion or thought for us. In our book club eight women read the same book however the interpretations are so diverse I wonder if we have read the same passage. It is because each of us operates from unique software programs that has downloaded different problem solving skills, beliefs, intentions, emotions, and physical abilities compiled in different formats from the person sitting beside you. An individual's reasoning and conclusions are reached from different internal dialogues and emotional patterns that have shaped a personality. Isn't it such a beautiful miracle how truly magnificent each person is? Each life has unique purpose and meaning manifesting into reality yet most of life will unfold in accordance with forces outside of our control. We ask questions of why life brings us pain and suffering and why is this part of the human experience.

Why do we go through difficult challenges causing turmoil and unrest? Are there reasons we face problems in relationships? Is free will and choice part of God's plan for our spiritual growth? Some of us openly search for answers, others are afraid to seek truth or do not care to know, that is to say all that we seek or shy away from is also part of a personal journey. Inner growth issues sometimes overwhelm us leading us to others for advice or counselling to solve or reconcile what is keeping us unhappy. In reality, truth is no psychiatrist, counsellor or drug will solve the problem for you; professional sessions can only guide you to find a solution as in the end you were the one who found the answer to your problem. Dependence on others while seeking to understand complexities of life can have exhausting, disappointing, short term results. I know it sounds harsh especially when you feel low but no one can mend emotional feelings and mental thoughts as effectively as you yourself. If you don't live life, life will live you. Instead of wandering willy-nilly dealing with consequences you may not wish, be the driver aiming for fruitful results. We don't have to continue living with burdening negative thoughts or depressed feelings but we do have to take responsibility for choices that led us to depression and present circumstances. We must be accountable for thoughts in the present moment for desired change to occur. Whether you are the victim or the creator of circumstance you must be involved in healing what pushes you away from a centered balanced state of being. Balanced state of being means living without extremes, yin and yang. If you look at a yin yang symbol the two halves have a lovely curve in the center where the two fit together symbolizing balance in the center. We cannot be "so happy it hurts" all the time or "so sad I can't breathe" all the time but knowing life swings us back and forth and resting in the calm center as an observer filtering extremes passing through instead of clinging on allows us to have healthier conscious thought. Digging deep within our psyche and hearts to discover the origins of negative burdens and finding the appropriate esoteric tool for assistance allows one to move forward with knowledge in hand towards healing the disturbance.

In the coming chapters I share with you a method for tapping into your inner power and how to connect to the all-knowing eternal source for the purpose of regaining confidence, understanding and resolution for ongoing life issues that move you away from a centered, balanced state of harmony. Finding "tools" for self-help is essential and one of the most powerful is energy healing for subtle bodies within the human field. A crucial first step is awareness of imbalance interrupting mental peace, emotional joy and physical wellness. Personally, I have found the way for coping with the darker heavier moments of life has been to be quiet and listen in stillness to the wisdom and guidance coming through prayer and meditation from an unseen all powerful source.

By listening carefully and ignoring the push and pull from ego and will power, the loving intelligence never steers me in the wrong direction.

It is from this well of all- knowing eternity that I have drawn strength to persevere and fulfill my destiny.

Events of life continue whether we are ready or not to deal with them when they present, but how we choose to handle adversity and what our spiritual belief systems are, contribute to our reality. It is personal choice how each of us reacts to negative issues we encounter and thoughts we create around any given situation.

Thoughts are energy in creation as thoughts become our individual reality moment by moment. By our thoughts we can positively manifest beautiful creations and feelings of euphoria or plan disparaging actions from feeling anger or sadness.

Perception of my reality will differ from yours depending on a myriad of influences, intentions and personal history that make each one of us unique.

What I do know for sure is that Life is about Love and bringing balance for receiving and giving love to all things without conditions or expectations. When we are in a state of feeling and intending love our most creative forces occur.

Science now shows us our heart responds to the outer world first by sending a wave of energy and information to the brain which sends messages throughout the body which responds in the reverse order for action. Your heart is made of subtle delicate energy that few come to recognize. You definitely are the experience of your heart. The heart closes from painful past unresolved energy patterns where everything feels negative because it is experienced through depressed, blocked energy before it has a chance to reach consciousness.

If we give and receive love unconditionally our heart energy center remains open flowing with healthy abundant life force. This creates balance on all levels and we can then say we are in a state of peace.

It is the ebb and flow of love that helps us to learn how to create balance from our inventory of experiences encountered from childhood.

There is no one that can rescue us from what each of us needs to experience for personal growth in a lifetime.

The more you listen to your inner voice and intuition the wiser you will become; in essence this is your soul trying to guide you through what you came to manifest in this lifetime.

Agreements are made in spirit before incarnation. A host of angels attend nearby with the sole purpose of enabling those agreements to manifest into our lives. Outcomes are never certain due to free will and choices we make along the way.

135

It took half a lifetime for me to accept the existence of spiritual guides. Simeon introduced himself as a spiritual guide during this lifetime and the impression or feeling is that we knew each other in a previous life during biblical times. I have visions of his appearance and feel his presence often but he assures me it is forbidden for those in spirit to interfere except for trying to introduce a thought or clarify an idea during times we are searching for direction. Due to free will each one of us ultimately makes the choice. Angels and spirit guides may be around us but in order to receive guidance you must ask, hence the truth of the biblical phrase "Ask and ye shall receive."

Addiction

A major problem in our society is an attitude of social acceptance to alcohol consumption.

The years of my first marriage were spent in a dysfunctional alcoholic relationship. I was young and consumed with work and raising a daughter. I could not depend on Keith for stability in any area of life.

Anger, resentment, fear, exhaustion, hurtful, deception, and dishonest are words to describe life during those years. It is no wonder all of that negativity manifested into physical ailments in my body. I was not able to give and receive love in a state of harmony closing myself off from the flow of universal life energy. All I could think of in those days was how to cope and how to escape my life.

Although I attended meetings, joined groups and received counseling for living with an alcoholic none solved problems for me, Keith or Kimberlee. It did provide the necessary information and insight for understanding the chaos created by the dysfunctional relationship.

When your heart is wounded you live in hope that someone can help you, and the harsh reality of knowing you are on your own deepens the feelings of isolation and despair.

The truth about addiction is; no one can change or influence an addict to get the help they need unless they are ready and desire change themselves. Chemical changes in the brain are so immense that the person is transformed into an unreasonable, unmanageable, dysfunctional being.

The brain no longer thinks logically or feels emotion as a normal person would. Addiction creates behaviors masking the emotion and anxiety the addict is trying to avoid by sedation through substance abuse.

There is falsehood in stating the cause of addiction lies entirely in childhood influences or a person's past; an alcoholic drinks because they like it.

That was my biggest mistake the first time. I kept trying to fix what was broken but in reality no one can be fixed unless they choose it.

Emotions run a gamut when living with addiction. Anger and hopelessness turn you upside down.

I remember joining a self-help group looking at weary faces expressing burnt out emotions thinking numbness meant survival. I wanted to shake them awake to see the truth that living in daily uncertainty can make you crazy and it is okay to be pissed off.

Behaviors from addicts are not acceptable when life becomes unmanageable for you. No one can tell you the best direction or guide your steps for gaining control of life as they are not living in your circumstances and each relationship with addiction is different. For a while I bought into the belief that if I changed it may help my husband's addictive personality. Educating myself with new information about the disease and its impact on families and countless heartbreaking testimonials certainly brought profound change in me.

In a moment of clarity I realized, wait a minute, I did not create this problem, I am not responsible for his drinking, I am the one suffering while holding life together, and he is the one needing to seek help for addiction.

You do need help getting out of the blaming cycle as bad stuff has been dumped in your lap festering injustice, but you are only responsible for your actions and seeking strength to accept what you cannot change.

Sometimes unknowingly or unconsciously we seek compassionate personalities to assist us during times we are overwhelmed by a growth lesson. The state of helplessness is avoidance to face the lessons.

For all of the women, men and young adults who are presently walking through a dark hour the question of why may not be revealed in the present moment but seeking answers in the outside world will not yield all truths either.

You may feel you have no choices but you always do. You may be challenged to dig deeper within yourself than ever before for solutions, truths and direction. It may be basic survival for yourself and children that push you towards change but do not hesitate one more day to appreciate the great divine being you are, the potent power you have within to move one step forward towards a place of joyful wisdom and peaceful heart.

We are all drivers in life and our choices steer us in different directions, at times veering us away from our path.

Nowhere is it written that we cannot choose yes or no, right or wrong, peace or war, anger or happiness, love or hate. The consequences we live with are from choices made whether or not they are good or bad.

Empowered by knowledge and awareness of emotions and thoughts will help you to make choices for the direction you want your life to lead.

Denial by the addict and family perpetuates disaster and if you are not aware of the manipulative personality pattern of addiction you become the enabler or rescuer essentially robbing the person from proceeding with what is meant to be. You cannot keep them safe from harm, poor health, embarrassment, or self-destruction. They are on a dark path for as long as it takes. Some may turn back by their own will to the joys of living but we must accept the addict may never make that choice.

The addict despises how they hurt others but the overwhelming desire to find relief from anxiety trumps atonement until sobriety is achieved.

It is the hardest yet most loving thing to allow an addict to find their bottom in order to return to a real life. You cannot fix what is broken.

Observation shows some people would rather avoid feelings that force them to face soul issues preferring a substance that offers temporary relief of emotional

139

discomfort, hence the astronomical growth of addictions in the world.

Alcohol ravages rational thinking creating chaos as the alcoholic manipulates situations in their life for re-fuelling and perpetuating their rationale for needing the next drink.

Once you accept this as truth only then can you effectively help yourself and loved ones. There is nothing you have done or ever will do that makes an alcoholic choose to have the next drink.

The addict is stuck and consumed but you must find a way to go on and live your life. It takes time to heal and you may be left with unresolved issues but caring for your needs with a desire for joyful living, letting go of the pain and dysfunction, in time brings peace.

No matter how unfair the feeling initially, accepting this as part of your life experience needed for soul growth allows reverence to enter.

Challenging yourself to not let bitterness and anger dominate your future brings awareness to personal inner power; after all you have gone through do you really need negative emotions to manifest into physical ailments; because it most definitely will be the result.

Healing in the present moment comes when you can accept your relationship with the addict through an open heart, loving unconditionally and understanding no matter the outcome you are not responsible for their addiction. It is seeing the "bigger picture" of this soul without placing conditions to influence the feeling of simply, purely, loving another being where there is no personality or deeds done to direct the state of love.

It is peeling away the layers of being human with understanding this person is part of your experience in the ballet of life assisting you to meet your goals in this carnation. It is seeing the inner core of someone; the light, love, truth of their soul, NOT the physical personality.

It is lovingly accepting **all** in your network of friends and family as souls of light who have joined in the orchestrated play and creative illusion of your life.

If you believe in reincarnation and karma it is understood if you have not learned the lesson meant for you, life will continue to bring the same circumstance over and over until you grow through experience into enlightenment. Faces may change but the experience will repeat itself giving you as many opportunities as necessary.

Karma is neither bad nor good; it is simply the experience you have created. It is the law of cause and effect in which you shape your life by choices you make.

The Universe can only respond to what you are creating, thinking, choosing; "your wish is my command." Gary Zukav reminds us the all-knowing intelligence does not decipher its responses by emotional decision alone, it can only deliver into your life what your intentions and focused thoughts and emotions are creating.

When we create with good thoughts and intentions we open ourselves to the human experience of learning, and interacting with others to be more compassionate, understanding, and loving.

As parents, we know our teenage children could be saved from a lot of misery and heartache if they would only listen to advice of what we already know will be the outcome in several circumstances. It is frustrating knowing we can help our children or friends in situations we recognize as imbalance but if that individual is not ready in their time frame of inner growth or open for receiving help, we must lovingly support them in their journey with non-interference.

When John and I reunited and lived in such happiness no one could have convinced me alcohol would show up in such a devastating way once again. Initially my old patterns of reaction took over and replayed with predictable conclusion.

Frustration from alcohol systematically destroying John's and my life together left me determined to find a new solution. Why was this happening once again? What is it I am to learn about addiction in this lifetime? Is there something about me that attracts an addictive personality? Even as a child I had exposure to tragedies revolving around alcohol that left their impressions. It was as though the universe had aligned experiences that I must go through in order to figure this out in this lifetime. Had John and I really agreed to this life lesson in spirit before we were born? I took inventory and searched within myself for answers. John is the kindest and most loving person I know and we had lived so happily together so why was this tragedy manifesting ten years later? The one constant grounding factor was my feeling of love for John no matter how it continued to be tested. The question I asked myself again and again, was I loving John unconditionally? I was not. I had not let go of wanting to fix or control the outcome of a situation as ego and will power took over my thoughts. I sat in the seat of judgment determining I was right and he was wrong. I guess like many my ego felt the need to be right and did not want to relinquish power. Having lived through one marriage with addiction I became independent and withdrawn into a self-righteous cocoon. In a sense neither of us had reached rock bottom. I was angry and disappointed that at the worst times of my life when I really needed love and support he could not be there for me as alcohol left him emotionally paralyzed.

During the last week before his accident when John drank day and night, due to my own emotional exhaustion from the recent tragedy of losing Ryan, I finally gave up and let go, feeling totally powerless to John's addiction. I even accepted John may die. I felt helpless and immense sadness but accepted John in his tragic state feeling love and sorrow in my heart, one soul to another.

Truths

Relationships with others bring the greatest opportunity for soul growth. We are not here simply to exist. Life is a gift, love, joy and a healthy body is a gift, problems and challenges are a gift because they make us insightful, wise, and kindhearted as we grow spiritually with each learning experience. I read once that God lives and grows through us and our experiences; we are part of God, we come from the oneness and share everything as whole spiritual energy.

Prayer gains power through focused thoughts in times when we are feeling extremely vulnerable or deeply touched. When we pray we reconnect to the oneness; God. Wayne Dyer says prayer is a meditation of emotion expressing our deepest wishes or gratitude. Prayer from conception has always been our way to connect to the universal mind reminding us that we are not alone. It is the oldest form of channeling or connecting to another frequency of energy.

I learned about the power of healing with loving intention in the early eighties while working in dentistry. It was by accident after a difficult surgery that I instinctively placed my hands over the area. Often I had pondered the purpose of perceiving information, many times ignoring the feelings or visions while standing beside someone, but on this day my hands were guided before any thought could prevent action. It was like a spirit guide became impatient thrusting me into motion. I felt empathy and desire to ease their pain and noticed intense heat in my hands as bleeding ceased and the person relaxed and calmed. I began placing my hands on patients who were extremely fearful to relax them and always after extractions.

It was rare that patients had bruising, swelling or complications. I never said a word but somehow an unspoken communication with the patient occurred.

My brother had a perforated ear drum from childhood and had undergone two previous skin grafts that were unsuccessful. On his third operation I asked if I could lay my hands on his ear as he came out of surgery. I sat visualizing the healing process and tissue repair as my hands tingled and heated over the area. His doctor remarked he had healed amazingly fast and was free to go and dive to his heart's content.

I felt inspired to continue, so each opportunity that came along I quietly used my hands for healing all the while aware of an increased intensity of heat while focusing and aligning my intention towards wellness. I did not dare tell anyone, remember this was 1982 and people had not awakened to accept energy healing yet, well, not a lot of people in Calgary.

I understood there is a greater power around us and felt humbled to be a pathway for this beautiful energy. We are all living conduits for healing energy whether we are conscious of our ability to channel or not.

In our realm of existence we determine everything by our five senses, as separate pieces of information but when channeling it is a whole energetic impression.

I am clear we live together in communities to assist, support and heal each other; that individual personal energy is part of a larger God energy.

We seem to ignore ancient wisdom of healing practices our forefathers utilized in daily life even suppressing intuitive and inherent knowledge of its existence placing it in the category of myth and folklore.

So much has been passed down by word or legends by great energy healers from past civilizations yet we choose to wait for the approval of science before we believe.

Instead we depend on the outer world and to heal our wounds rather than going within ourselves and reconnecting to the promised creative energy for helping us to live well.

We are designed to heal ourselves if our bodies are provided with the proper tools as genetically we were created to sustain life, however through interference we have damaged our food source by chemicals the body has no predisposition to assimilate or eliminate.

We are amazed how our physical bodies miraculously heal from injuries visible to the eye, but have little faith in healing we cannot see.

Although we have been conditioned to look in our outer world for healing, we are magnificent powerful beings of energy that can bring about immense change at a subatomic level through our intentions, heartfelt feelings and mind-full thoughts.

"Because life molds the outer world to reflect the inner arrangement of our minds, there is no way of bringing about the outer perfection we seek other than by the transformation of ourselves. There is nothing to change but our concept of self.

As within; so without." Neville.

For years during healing sessions impressions presented physical conditions that could be aided synergistically with herbal medicines in the healing process.

In the spring of 2005 I began receiving a different frequency during channeling sessions. The new frequency tuned me directly into the emotional level of the body intensely focusing energy at that layer of the human field. Emotional and mental disturbances in one's field manifest into physical conditions creating imbalance and disease if blocked long enough therefore all three areas must be considered in treatment.

Healing past and present misunderstandings through awareness of thought and acceptance of feeling opens a channel for forgiveness and love.

When we become aware of how negative emotions are felt in areas of our body a powerful shift takes place in our mental health as well. We begin to understand we can take control of present conditions by solving upsets and disallowing them to control us. Physical conditions begin to disappear rapidly with minimal herbal remedy needed.

It became clear to me that healing had shifted its focus for mankind and through healing our emotions and mental misconceptions we would find physical healing and direction towards wellness. The cautionary note here is to be aware of emotional and mental imbalances striving to correct them before the matrix within the human energy field manifest into physical states. Many symptoms present before physical matter has permanently changed within the body. Once a fully blown disease becomes reality everything changes, requiring allopathic and naturopathic treatments complemented by an individual's self-healing power. Spirit, mind and body work together as a whole unit and when one of the three moves to an extreme, away from center, the other two will eventually follow suit.

Past Life

During this same year I received a vision that finally put the pieces together from the previous dream I had at age fifteen. It began by telling of an area in Wales that long ago was named "angels be" and now goes by the name Anglesey. This village was once the envy of several surrounding villages creating discord and physical clashes. "Angelsbe" had an advanced life style offering cooperative growing methods to feed its citizens but more importantly knowledge of healing the sick. Neighboring tribes would kidnap men from the village who were known healers to learn of their methods or powers, but the healers were sworn to secrecy for the greater good of their people and suffered at the hands of their captors.

Healers continued to disappear over a long period in history, taking its toll on the health and morale of citizens, adversely affecting the entire village.

Villagers feared losing their healers and sacred wisdom so decided to pass the information onto the eldest daughter of each family.

She would be taken aside and trained in ancient ways of healing swearing to never reveal what had been passed down by her forefathers. This change was adopted insuring health care for many generations from the first born daughter in each family. Even as warring between villages continued Angelsbe prospered and thrived as a successful community for a long time.

The Great War that destroyed this village was a bloody slaughter. Most of its people did not survive and those that did fled far away to blend in with other villages. The healers that survived were afraid to expose themselves and because there were no written records it was feared "the knowledge" was lost.

Many years passed after the Great War and the inhabitants of Angelsbe had spread far and wide into different regions

147

but strangely with no teachings the first born daughter in many families would show interests in herbal medicines and healing practices. Although several centuries have passed and many continents have distanced the original inhabitants, to this day inherent healing knowledge shows up in many descendants from this area. They are usually drawn to natural healing methods having an easy understanding of how the human body and plants work synergistically, and may be the first born daughter in the family.

This glimpse of a past life experience was in a sense comforting, answering many questions about present day life.

As I continued travelling back in time during this vision another mystery around gathering places of raised stones such as Stonehenge became clear. The placement of the mammoth stones created a star like reflection during two spring and fall full moons. At this time in history these stones contained a mineral acting like a solar battery.

They absorbed the suns energy and when the full moon shone directly on the stones they began glowing, reflecting long beams of light into the surrounding fields.

This was considered to be a sacred time for planting and harvesting as the work continued far into the night during the shining moon. Seeds planted within the glowing beams of light would yield the strongest, healthiest crops.

Whole communities would gather for this time of work and celebration and couples who were trying to conceive or the sick that needed healing would either lie or lean upon the stones receiving the healing energy emitted.

Everyone experienced a feeling of rejuvenation inside the circle of stones from vibrations of energy radiating outward.

Great feasts, music and ceremony took place throughout day and night during these times of full moon.

Throughout history it was believed these sites were used only for sun worship, however it seems the moon played a very important role as well. There will come a day that science will find evidence of this mineral unusually high in concentration in the stones found around these formations. Pieces of stone that broke away may be buried under layers of earth that still create changes in energy vibrations during certain times of the year.

Channeled Message

On Earth Day, 2009, I sat in meditation channeling the following: My question was directed towards changes in communication as we approach the foretold "Golden Age". The response was; now is a time to remain open and receptive to messages coming from the superconscious mind; our soul energy where true power lies. Now, in present time of mankind's evolution we must practice and prepare through meditation for connecting to the spiritual plane for knowledge and guidance as we wander from the era of written word towards intuitive inspired intelligence. I was shown a beautiful vision of my soul rising through the crown chakra melting from physical form into flowing energy for reconnecting with spiritual family. The energetic self is luminescent pearl white and indescribable brightness of swirling colors and densities. I was aware of rising upward far above my physical body into a black void. This space was full of love and total knowledge, completeness. In this higher vibration there is no such thing as time between questions and answers, it just is.

I observed my transformation from a bright white orb into an expanded and illuminated being sending intense beams of light into the darkness in all directions. The illuminated space was brilliant, beautiful, loving and peaceful and my heightened awareness observed lovely beings gathered in a circle. I felt emotionally whole in the immensity of love surrounding and passing through me. I listened, floating in the center of my light as they explained this place is where we (everyone) could meet in communion. My thoughts rambled in the realm of quantum physics feeling an explanation that dark matter is the sum of conscious thought and intense emotion which create density, movement and expansion between physical spaces. Thoughts and emotions are energy creating constant change in the universe.

If we desire we can always communicate into the spiritual plane using our higher level of consciousness. In this higher vibration of love and light you are able to enter into communion with your higher self and elevated souls serving humanity.

We have always inherently known this eternal source but through spiritual repression and disconnection most of mankind has buried its memory.

There are sentinels who walk amongst us holding steady to a light of love ready to help us re- connect to the world of spirit as we continue our quest for balance between the physical and spiritual realms. In this vibration we can ask our questions, replenish our souls, and seek guidance. We never need to feel alone with our problems.

I asked for further explanation of the angelic gateway and with loving humor an explanation was given that the inspiration to build a gateway was not for the angels, but "us", for reaching a place of communion. Some feel the need for a physical portal to access the etheric plane. There are presently many souls on Earth for meeting the necessary increased vibration of Earth's energy grid. A faster vibration is needed for speeding up time as too much destruction has occurred too quickly and cleansing of the earth is essential. Much human energy is manifested into critical knowledge during this time needed to bring about earthly repair and healing. As we approach the end of this cycle, during the transition, there will be great loss and chaos to endure causing a retreat of many souls, leaving a less populated yet peaceful, loving community to continue the journey of assisting Mother Earth's healing. It was explained there is much change taking place presently in the Universe and other dimensions and we are but a blip of this expanding Universal time.

Many unexplained physical symptoms people experience are due to energetic frequency changes taking place in the realignment of energy fields around the Earth.

Earth is wrapped in a magnetic field affected by changes constantly occurring between the sun, moon and earth. Animals navigate and use this field, our sixth sense taps into magnetic fields as experiments have proven two brains in separate locations on the earth can share the same information. Global consciousness affects the random number collector because we share earth's magnetic fields. More than usual electromagnetic interference from the Sun and gravitational pull from the Moon is occurring as other planets and moons align as we herald in this new age. The earth's magnetic poles will change as a result of the suns magnetic fields shifting causing magnetic field changes in all of the planets and moons within its solar system.

Many will experience personal energy centers (chakras) adjusting as human evolution awakens our brain to broader perception of conscious and super conscious realities during the great shift.

There is much fear and chaos in the hearts of mankind presently, due to belief systems in operation that pull us further away from our spiritual center. The emptiness, loneliness, creates a stuffing syndrome where people consume more food, clothes, and things, to fill what is lacking resulting in temporary satisfaction. Relationships are more needy, greater insecurities arise and better, more sex seems to be the fix all solution. The elusive feeling of wholeness and contentment gap widens without spiritual centeredness.

Once again we emphasize this is not an external shift of destruction for mankind even though there is physical change taking place within the earth, rather an internal shift that will begin to create a new reality. An extended hand in intention of Love reaches ten times in length energetically speaking.

We will notice a reversal shift from worldwide efforts of charity turning towards family and local community as revelations of charitable organized corruption reveals a greater need of bringing relief to those within our reach. Corrupted leaders leading their citizens into poverty by selfish greed will fall as conscious awareness rises to truth that no one is greater or lesser, we are created as equals.

For several years during channeling and meditation, messages were clear that we are moving quickly towards a shift in consciousness of mankind and it will create great chaos for those that remain stuck in old ways of thinking. In this new vibratory frequency those who can shift will feel lighter and be able to handle the frenetic changes mentally and physically occurring in daily life.

The density in this dimension we are living in now is fluctuating allowing more of us to connect to those souls passed into energetic form. The shift that is foretold lies in a rebirthing of consciousness for mankind from a third dimension into a higher faster dimension that requires creative shaping without history or concepts of future to influence the minute, hour or day we are presently living. It will force us to live in moment to moment awareness.

By December 21 2012 the Precession of the equinox will complete itself and a new cycle of another thirteen thousand years will be initiated. In February 2013 the Maya will perform the first ceremony of the new cycle and humanity will begin a rapid healing on earth by showing that love and caring is the new way of the world.

Enlightenment and understanding will blossom in many, enabling them to be pillars of strength throughout the world holding a steady calming light.

Fear will be pervasive in sustaining violence and anger around the world for those who cling tightly to material temptations.

Some will try very hard to prevent further disintegration of life as it was known but mankind will proceed into the lighter energy that operates with compassion, love and

153

wholeness. The physical body will experience more bone and muscle disturbances as the new vibration settles in and around us.

The earth's magnetic fields are shifting and will realign, in turn affecting the gravitational relationship we have with our moon and sun thus affecting our physical and mental bodies. According to scientists we are overdue for this occurrence as typically the fields shift every two hundred and fifty thousand years and we have not experienced a polar shift for seven hundred and fifty thousand years.

As prophesized, many souls will choose to exit from physical form during this shift. It is a time to be aware of any and all conflicts of a personal nature that require emotional healing in this lifetime.

Forgiveness and moving into a state of acceptance and love for each other will be necessary for the world as a whole to move forward through this evolutionary shift.

Realizing we are each a tiny part of a greater whole is now of immense importance for mankind and by shedding the smaller insignificant negative patterns of ego and will, no longer of service, will bring forth our salvation.

We need a mass of conscious thought free of ego to pray for a higher level of super consciousness to inspire mankind's awareness of God. To meditate of your own higher self is a direct link to the universal mind.

The song that I came to sing remains unsung to this day,
I have spent my days in stringing and unstringing my
instrument.
The time has not come true; the words have not been
rightly set;
Only there is the agony of wishing in my heart.

By Rabin Dranath Tagore

We must not let this state of wishing in our hearts enter
our lives, as there is much to do, say, and set right for our
souls. Let there be joy in the journey of discovery and
celebration in the hearts of all as we see our path more
clearly. It is not by accident that you have chosen to be
alive at this time in history and great change.
All life carries energy and intelligence that has a will to
manifest; each plant, insect, animal, and human has a
purpose and life cycle to complete deserving respect and
the right to just be. Humans evolve in their spiritual
growth the same way we grow from children into adults
maturing in our spiritual knowledge from life experience.
Let go and Let Live simply allows every living thing a
space to complete their personal expression.

"Let nothing, dear Lord disturb the silence of this moment
Let nothing disturb my focus as I enter into the truth that
this day of my life will never come again.
How shall I live my life today?"

By Caroline Myss

Energy and Vibration

Healing concepts are based on vibrations of one thing effecting the vibrations of another. If one thing is vibrating at a different rate in close proximity the two will naturally pull each other toward a balance.

This explains a concept reference to an "energy vampire." We have all experienced someone in our lives that after a visit we feel drained. If we could see what was happening, we would observe a lopsided energy field leaning and extending a hook energetically into our energy field pulling positive energy into their negative energy. The balance is created, they feel better and you wonder why you are feeling more drained when you had been feeling so great. It is very important to become aware of and make the connection to people and situations in life that affect you positively to remain in a faster and higher vibration state. At this level you feel healthier and happier and problems seem insignificant.

We each have our own vibrations that affect how we think and operate in life, and we are constantly bombarded by the vibrations of all living things around us.

Once you accept we are affected by an unseen world then you can make better choices for an environment that is healthy for you.

As healers raise their vibration held in purity, love, and intention of spirituality, it provides a healing effect on those they touch harmonizing areas of the body physically, mentally and emotionally. By holding this higher, faster level of energy on a person you provide them an opportunity for their body to shift into a higher vibration. As this removes blockages from condensed energy held in certain areas, their body responds by correcting itself.

A cascade of health occurs when our thoughts influence our mental state which in turn affects our emotional health that in time manifests into our physical body.

As we hold our feelings down in our body we block the flow of energy creating stagnation in body systems that can create disease in our physical state.

The human energy field is considered to be a fifth state of matter, bioplasmic, and matter in all forms is defined as condensed energy. Everything in our Universe is energy vibrating at a different frequency creating diverse densities and states of matter. Einstein said it best, "E = mc2" meaning there is no difference between matter and energy as both are made of all kinds of particles. If some particles stick together, that is matter but if they don't, that is energy. Bioenergetics studies the energy flow through living systems. Life requires free available energy and living systems make use of living energy. You are an amalgamation of complex energy fields co-existing with the universe. Science now shows that as a supernova explodes it sends particles of energy into the far reaching places of the universe. The smaller than atom particles called neutrinos blast through space and are part of all living systems. At any given moment we may have trillions of neutrinos passing through our body unaware of their existence. Disease is disorder in the bioenergetic field where the field is weak or congested. A therapist can feel differences in thickness, temperature, emptiness or lack of movement. A person's bioenergetic field naturally responds to channeled focused energy from a therapist who fills the deficits and clears congestion.

The human body produces a lot of energy for complicated anabolic and catabolic processes. We eat food that produces calories for metabolic energy. Each tiny cell has its own energy center called the mitochondria that produces ATP, cell fuel. The human body has inner organs and bones that must be protected. Ligaments and tendons connect bone to muscle that covers and protects nerves and inner tissues.

A lot of energy flows throughout the body for maintaining

homeostasis but sometimes this magnificent organic machine falls into a weakened state and needs assistance to return to optimal health. Think of a car battery that has lost its charge and needs a boost. We run cables between the dead battery and a fully charged battery exchanging energy from one source to another. The result is a revitalized battery that is ready and charged to run the electrical needs of the car. The same takes place between an energy healer and weakened bodies whose energy levels are low and need boosting. For example, if muscle tissue has stiffened too much then instead of protecting nerves, organs and bone it impedes healthy blood flow and inflammation sets in resulting in pain. The knotted muscle needs manipulation to release built up lactic acid, improve circulation and return to a relaxed state. Inflammation is stagnated condensed energy in an area of the body where blood is pooling to heal the problem. Focused, directed energy from a bioenergetics therapist unblocks these areas re-establishing oxygenated blood flow to energize cells for optimal function once again. An energy healer has learned how to focus and direct energy for the purpose of helping living systems. Instead of scattered chaotic energy, a therapist can harness this force for a specific area or intentional purpose. Most typically a therapist will channel energy through the hands, normally felt as heat, tingling, or even a cooling sensation. Bioenergetics healing is deeply relaxing and harmonizing to the entire body.

It seems every decade a new discovery of healing with energy is born, each claiming to be the "best or strongest." Universal life force energy has been given many names by civilizations around the globe since the beginning of time. No original thought exists, all that is known resides in the universal mind patiently waiting to be accessed and brought into reality.

Body Field

Wherever you place your focus in your body field there is an immediate flow of energy stimulating cells in the corresponding area.

One can use the visual example of a bee sting. The pain from the sting brings your focus and attention immediately to the site of injury. As all of our senses are directed to this area, we observe the spot swelling with redness on the skin, stinging, throbbing pain, faster breathing, and emotions sending alarm hormones throughout the body for response action. The physical, mental and emotional bodies are simultaneously responding to the injury with intense focus.

It is also important to know where we feel our thoughts throughout our body. Stressful thoughts for some are felt in the stomach and described as "knots or butterflies" of nervous energy gathered in that area.

By changing our thoughts to love and gratitude we increase the vibration of our energy field allowing us to feel lighter and more positive. When feeling angry, sad or worn out by events of life we are vibrating at a lower frequency effecting all levels of our body field thereby weakening our physical state as energy is impeded in its flow in and around us.

It is at the slower vibration level that problems seem to engulf us. In higher frequencies we feel spiritually connected and content in knowledge that we are not alone.

Being aware of emotions or feelings you bring into the body as well as thoughts you focus on will affect your energy field and heart pulse wave sending out powerful messages throughout the body. Focusing your feelings on love and gratitude in the heart can bring about states of immense bliss in the physical body. Focused feelings of anger and hate bring states of tense muscle rigidity, cramps and exhaustion.

159

Everything in the physical world is constantly changing just as the seasons of spring and fall bring about renewal and decay. Even within our bodies we literally replace ourselves every two years as cells grow and die.

You can observe living energy fields on a beautiful bright sunny day by gazing into the sky studying small white orbs that seem to move rapidly in all directions. Sunlight excites and charges the globules causing them to move faster. At first I wondered what on earth I was looking at, even questioning whether they were wind swept seeds, but after further research was able to confirm they were indeed little energy orbs whizzing about.

Even the trees in your yard give off a glow along their outer edges.

Observe a branch, looking out from its edge just slightly and you will see a moving haze around the entire tree.

When observing energy fields around plants they most often emit a blue color on the outer edges of their leaves followed by a yellow/gold color that extends into a dull white edge of their field.

In contrast animals most often have white close to their bodies followed by a color extending out to the edge of their field, and humans have several layers of color in their field. Energy is about frequencies and all living things vibrate with energy frequencies that can be seen as the "aura" emitted by that particular entity.

Organic life vibrates and glows and if you cannot see it perhaps you can feel it by holding your hands slightly above the object you are studying while feeling for changes in heat or density surrounding the object. Try rubbing your hands together for about thirty seconds, and then slowly move them away from each other. You can feel a difference in heat as you pull your hands apart but also a magnetic attraction as you slowly bring them back together. You can also feel the heat and density in the space between your hands before they touch together.

Pretend you have a ball of energy between your hands and rotate it or rub the top of it and you will feel a subtle difference in heat and density.

Early spring brings the arrival of migrating birds looking for left over berries still lingering on tree branches.

The fermented berries leave birds helplessly drunk, flying into windows. The telltale thump brings my attention to peer out checking if one is down and needs assistance. The temperatures remain frigid during springtime in Calgary and when a bird becomes immobile they lose precious heat quickly. If a bird is stunned from impact it may recover quickly and be on its way but if it is knocked out it may die from hypothermia.

I grab a soft cloth and lay it over the bird as I scoop the wee creature into my hands. The bird is completely limp and unmoving and at times I fear it may be dead but I sit and visualize white healing light going through its little body until a faint stirring is felt.

I wait patiently using my hands as a warm incubator until there is strength in the bird's movement then gently remove its cover allowing the bird to fly when ready. I am rewarded by this little creature quietly looking up as it regains awareness and eventually flies away.

I have been mostly quiet and shy about energy healing for most of my life but feel Ryan saying it is time to let it be known that on the "other side" many are anxiously awaiting this next stage of mankind's evolution. He speaks about time space continuum (I do not fully grasp it) referring to what we call "the veil" as a different density we enter in another dimension. For example I saw his arm pushing through the "density" which appeared like a gel.

Sparks of glowing energy pulsated around the elastic gel-like matter but unable to penetrate the membrane, the gel bounced back to its original shape.

He insists time is short in relation to civilization as we

know it. Earth has never known complacency and true to its nature great change is soon to occur.

Ryan would love to bring peace to his father and mother in this place of communion, as we all desire to commune with loved ones who have passed over. I have had several conversations with Ryan since his death, all giving detail to what we term life after death. Ryan has little interest in discussing his earthly life from my many questions, explaining it was a small reference in the grander scheme of what is. Ryan states that questions asked cannot always be answered in a manner we expect as those souls passed over cannot interfere with our purpose or life path.

They cannot reveal answers that may affect our free will and choices we make that determine the outcome in life. They can only reveal information if it is for our greater good or the greater good for all. He went on to explain when in spirit thoughts create unlimited realities.

For instance, a soul thinks of someone passed over who appears in illusion form, and how a soul imagines a person from memory creates recognition no matter the actual physical appearance at death. In spirit if Ryan creates a visit with my dad they may show themselves to each other as young men instead of the many years of age difference in life.

Individual souls create illusions from earthly memory seeking familiar souls who choose to be part of the illusion but nothing is permanent and time is not a concept in spirit. In spirit we are energy identified by imprinted wisdom on our soul gained from previous incarnations but feelings experienced in the body are unique to the earthly plane.

There is no pain, sadness or negative emotions felt in spirit as in body, instead we become part of an all knowing intelligence that creates as a whole energy through immense nurturing love. Individuality is only on the earthly plane.

Elevated souls who have chosen to assist incarnated souls through non-interfering spiritual guidance are always present.

Edgar Cayce once said "do not fear conversation with the dead in dreams. If both participate, it may be an actual encounter of bodiless consciousness."

The intention for discussing how to connect to Universal energy for the purpose of channeling carries hope we can remove darkness by awakening the practice of healing with light yielding positive outcome in everyday life.

I believe as we realign with who we truly are collectively, a power will enter into the world bringing peace and harmony within ourselves, planet and universe to create greatness unlike any memory of mankind.

Meditation begins by being aware of what you are thinking, what you are feeling and how your physical body is responding to all of that.

Relax the body by sitting or lying down or by walking at a relaxed pace. Think of how you are breathing. Most of us are shallow breathers affecting the physiological response of inhaling, exchanging, and exhaling the oxygen and carbon dioxide we need.

By taking deep breaths in through the nose we allow little hairs to filter particles, and for air to be warmed before entering the lungs. A deep breath also means we are compressing the diaphragm which puts pressure on the vagus nerve that sends messages to the brain we are relaxed. Take a deep breath in through the nose filling the lungs fully. Pause, and then blow out the air through pursed lips making a swooshing sound.

After a few deep breaths you begin to notice how calm you feel. Once your breathing rhythm is established your mind will try to take over by rehashing every event of your life. Pick one word or thought that evokes a pleasant feeling so you can remain relaxed, perhaps repeating either peace or love.

Each time thoughts from your ego or will center tries to bully its way in, keep repeating your peace or love thought, breathing and relaxing. Meditation creates mindfulness in a sense that you let go of awareness of physical presence, joining together the sub-conscious and super conscious mind.

Listening to peaceful music, walking in nature, gardening, even daydreaming can bring us into a state of meditation.

It is a practice of patience and discipline that allows you to drift into a space integrated with eternal energy; present since creation.

A Meditation

Once upon a time long, long ago, in the beginning, Mother Earth nourished us and all things were good.

The air was clean, and moist, the sky was so blue, so clear we could see great distances.

Brilliant colored birds of red, orange, yellow, green, and blue glided pristine currents as songs of playful melody rang through the air.

Cascading waterfalls splashed and gurgled into pools of refreshing life giving water. Pools emptied into streams, and streams into brooks trickling in the flow of life.

Flowers of dazzling color bloom in grasses, trees, beside the brooks, streams and ponds. Their fragrance blend in heavenly aroma of sun kissed breezes.

Fruits, all shapes and color grew in abundance in lush green trees and bushes. The fruits are ripe, sweet, juicy and nourishing.

Healing plants surround us for well-being, just look at them all!

You carry this inherent knowledge within.

Remember the herbs, roots, and flowers for healing thyself.

Know you can find healing from what Mother Earth provides.

Feel the connection to creation within, as you are a beautiful part of the source.

Your heart sits in your body the same degree as Earth sits on its axis.

Salty blood runs through you just as salty oceans run through Mother Earth.

Fresh water brings us to life just as it brings life to every living thing on Earth.

We are a living matrix of Mother Earth.

Now, relax, deeply breathe in peace, and let yourself feel warm, nourished, balanced and loved, and you feel so good.

The Field

The human energy field is considered to be a fifth state of matter. To feel your own field extend your arms out to the side of your body with palms facing upward. Take a few deep breaths, close your eyes and slowly begin raising your arms over your head keeping them fully extended until the finger tips touch. Let your arms descend slowly with palms facing down while you feel for changes on the perimeter of your field. In other words your own energy field surrounds you like an oval egg and with practice you can perceive it by changes in heat or density in the perimeter of your field.

To understand our energy field further we need to include the seven major energy centers referred to as chakras. Dr. David Tansley, a radionics specialist states, the seven major chakras are formed at points where standing lines of light cross each other twenty one times. The standing lines are often referred to as meridians of energy around our body. We also have twenty one minor chakras and the two located in the palms of the hands are important for directing healing energy.

Energy flows into all of the chakras from the Universal energy field by vortices that appear like whirlpools or hurricanes sucking energy inward.

Barbara Brennan's research finds a normal open chakra is about six inches in diameter sitting about an inch from the body and when in harmony swirls in a clockwise direction. The more energy we let flow, the healthier we are. Illness is caused by an imbalance or a blocking of the flow.

There is a vertical flow of energy that pulsates up and down the spine with tips of the chakras pointing in so that we are receiving energy from above and grounding energy from Mother Earth.

Chakras have a front and back where energy flows in and out all the time under normal conditions.

The fronts and backs of chakras are related to feelings and will centers. Each chakra is associated with an endocrine gland and major nerve plexus. The relationship of physical symptoms to these areas helps us to understand illness in corresponding locations and also indicates where emotions or mental concepts are out of balance. When you are aware of tension you can feel it in the chakra associated with the part of the body feeling the stress. The word chakra means wheel in Sanskrit. Chakras are spinning energy centers located along the spine meridian. Each Chakra vibrates at an orderly sequence of seven vibrations at a certain frequency. Colors of the spectrum of light represent seven vibrations with the longest wave length, red, at the bottom and the lightest, pale violet, at the top.

By exploring our energy field we may rediscover with high sense perception all that we need for living in healthy balance.

We are blessed having unlimited access to knowledge from an energetic library since the inception of time; we just need to rediscover the code buried inside us all along to enter. Awareness and a desire to learn is the first step.

The Chakras

Each one of the major chakras has a color and a sound that assists in balancing the vibration and frequency of that center. Stones and essential oils are also used for balancing the vibration and frequency of chakras.

First chakra, Earth, is the Root or base center associated with physical sensation and functioning, foundation and sense of survival. Its color is red, stones used are red carnelian, garnet or ruby, the sound is made by the C note or vowel AA or Sanskrit sound LAM; the essential oil is myrrh representing healing. The corresponding body area is the adrenals, spinal column and kidneys.

Visualizing red energy increases physical strength in muscles and improves circulation.
I am grounded and supported.

Second chakra, Water, is the Sacral or pelvic center associated with creativity, love and passion for others.
Its color is orange, stones used are orange carnelian, or orange calcite, the sound is made by the D note or vowel A or Sanskrit sound VAM; the essential oil is jasmine representing happiness, self-awareness and self-esteem.
The corresponding body area is the gonads and reproductive system. Visualizing orange energy stimulates the nervous system and supports vitality.
I am creative and connected

Third chakra, Fire, is the Solar plexus center associated with action, will, chi, and spiritual wisdom, consciousness of life and knowledge of our place in the universe. Its color is yellow, stones used are amber or yellow calcite, the sound is made by the E note or vowel E or Sanskrit sound RAM; the essential oil is juniper representing peace.
The corresponding body area is the pancreas, stomach, liver, gall bladder, and nervous system. Visualizing yellow/gold energy protects our core nerve plexus and lifts us up as a ray of sunshine.
I am one with the Universe.

Fourth chakra, Air, is the heart center associated with giving and receiving love for humanity and life. Its color is green, stones used are aventurine or emerald, the sound is made by the F note or vowel I or Sanskrit sound YAM; the essential oil is bergamot representing creativity and self-esteem.
The corresponding body area is the thymus, heart, blood, vagus nerve, and circulatory system.

Visualizing green energy promotes healing, quieting, cooperation and renewal.
I give and receive unconditional love.

Fifth chakra, Sound, is the throat center associated with communication, the power of word, speaking the truth, taking responsibility for our actions, sense of self, devotion and listening. Its color is sky blue; stones used are lapis lazuli, blue sodalite, or angelite.
The sound is made by the G note or vowel O or Sanskrit sound HAM; the essential oil is chamomile representing joy, and peace.
The corresponding body area is the thyroid, vocal cords, and lungs. Visualizing blue energy stimulates, calms, and clears thought processes.
I speak my truth clearly and kindly

Sixth chakra, Light, is the brow or third eye center associated with wisdom, protecting and nurturing life, capacity to visualize concepts and ability to carry out ideas. Its color is indigo or purple; stones used are apatite, opal or lapis, the sound is made by the A note or vowel U or Sanskrit sound OM; the essential oil is thyme representing alertness.
The corresponding body area is the pituitary, lower brain, left eye, ears, and nose. Visualizing purple energy strengthens ambition and determination that is related to will power.
My mind is open to divine wisdom.

Seventh chakra, Consciousness, is the crown center associated with knowing our higher selves and spiritual aspects of mankind, divine angelic guidance. Its color is violet or white; stones used are amethyst, or clear quartz, the sound is made by the A note or vowel U or Sanskrit sound OM; the essential oil is lavender representing contentment and restfulness.

The corresponding body area is the pineal, upper brain and right eye. Visualizing violet energy promotes recovery from illness and raises the vibration towards a higher spiritual frequency. I am one with the infinite, my higher self.

Two other colors to visualize for wellbeing are pink which represents the energy of love and goodwill towards others for the creation of harmony.

Silver promotes growth as a nourishing energy and increases sensitivity to people and environment while decreasing emotionalism.

The Seven Major Chakras and the areas they cover

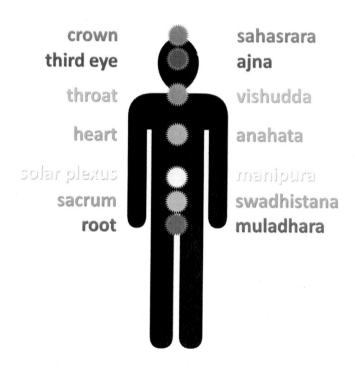

crown   sahasrara
third eye   ajna
throat   vishudda
heart   anahata
solar plexus   manipura
sacrum   swadhistana
root   muladhara

Sound Therapy

During a healing session a person is in a relaxed state and receptive to sound which provides nourishment for the subtle bodies. Sound affects the mind and body as the essence of sound is vibration. Music played in a certain key vibrates a particular chakra affecting the way we feel when that music is played. Each person has a distinct frequency; sometimes forming disharmony, therefore balancing frequencies through sounds creating vibrations within the physical and subtle bodies can be very powerful. Sounds emitted by Crystal or Tibetan bowls create vibrations and frequencies which can be felt throughout the body. The human body is made largely of fluid that is affected by sound waves similar to waves we see in the fluid of a crystal wine glass when a finger rubs the rim. We ourselves can use breath and voice to harmonize physical and subtle bodies through sounds. Each time we take a breath and form the sound of OM or A for example it is felt in our body as a balancing vibration. Take a deep breath in and slowly begin the sound dragging the Ooooo to Mmmm. When you have found the correct pitch for yourself, your field, it will feel as though the breath continues forever. Experiment whether it is a low or high pitch that feels best, you will know because it feels like perfect balance in your body, like the sound belongs there, and effortless breath that goes on and on. Can you imagine how great we would feel each day if we had an energetic work out as well as physical exercise? All the vowel or Sanskrit sounds representing the seven major chakras have a higher or lower pitch, usually noticed as deep base throated sound in the root chakra. The pitch rises to soprano as you ascend towards the crown chakra. After you have intoned each sound separately then join them from low to high and high to low in one breath to complete the exercise.

Sit back and notice the smile on your face and the peace you feel inside along with a joyful attitude to begin the day. We are bombarded with a variety of sound in our environment, some unpleasant which is termed as noise. The brain is a master at tuning out background noise for us to maintain sanity but studies have shown certain sounds can incite anger and aggression while others instill relaxation and peace. For comparison sake use water as an experiment and see how you feel when you hear booming sounds from crashing ocean waves against rock compared to the snap crackle sound of the wave retreating over the sand. How do you feel when you hear water trickling through a small brook, lapping on the lakeshore, gushing through river rapids, a descending waterfall or a dripping faucet? Sound can be energizing, calming or distracting. Think about what kind of sound you want to fill your space when you have a choice. Do you want sound to energize or sound to relax you?

Preparing to Connect

Each person will discover a method for connecting with the field that feels comfortable. I was intuitively drawn to the following method and found in the beginning I struggled to relax mind and body when entraining but eventually re-connection felt like stepping forward into a place of comfort. Relaxing enough to clear our mind from nagging thoughts is a huge road block in the beginning, making us aware of constant mental chatter. Our inner voice loves to have power and can either be our friend or enemy but never likes to be quiet. It constantly communicates with us offering opinions, decisions, ideas or impressions of everything we do even if unasked. Stillness of our conscious mind takes practice and moment by moment awareness, for in a nano second it interrupts the gap of silence we strive for. During channeling people will claim a feeling of being in a familiar place accompanied by heightened awareness and feelings of well-being. Although channeling does require disciplined focus and concentration, people are able to channel far more easily than they expect. Common sensations are heat and tingling and you may notice changes in your posture or breathing or feel a vibratory presence. Some feel as if they are floating or see lights and colors as they perceive a higher vibration. When you start to channel you may be surprised that a verbal message, inner message or mental picture comes through to you but relax and trust that sometimes the most obvious wisdom is truth in simple form. On two occasions I channeled the most beautiful composition of sounds from what had to be angelic origin and tears flowed from the overwhelming vibration I felt. The sounds emitted were foreign; it was somewhat startling particularly since I am not a vocalist. Have faith that what comes through will assist you or another in creating higher wisdom in the world as messages manifest into physical reality.

When seeing clients for healing sessions begin the day by taking inventory of how your body is feeling or what it requires for nourishment and well-being. Follow a stretching routine to remove tension in muscles or structure areas. Take inventory of mental thoughts and emotional feelings to determine if there is anything you are holding onto presently.

Depending on that information you may choose the above tools discussed under chakras, for assisting in clearing and balancing the chakras and field. I personally prefer using Sanskrit sounds for clearing as I am very sensitive how sound changes vibration in each chakra.

A blend of seven essential oils diffused into the air or mixed in water and misted above the head creates links to emotional memory in the limbic center of the brain, stimulated by smell. Scents of essential oils representing the seven chakras assist in reconnecting emotional thoughts held in corresponding chakra centers.

I find it useful to mist the essential oil blend into the energy field before and after sessions for assisting awareness and recall of emotions and memories.

Before beginning a session I pray for guidance, love, truth, and healing. I run my hands about two inches above the body over the seven centers feeling for density, speed and strength of movement in each one. Place an appropriate stone on each center; for example a green aventurine on the fourth or heart chakra, blue sodalite on the fifth or throat chakra and so on. Placing a clear quartz crystal in the person's left hand increases the pulse of energy and a rose quartz crystal in their right hand calms anxiety and nervous tension.

A larger piece of unpolished amethyst is placed about six inches from the crown chakra as an aid for spiritual focus.

Before channeling, a "generator" quartz crystal pendulant

is held about two inches above each of the seven chakras. It is very helpful in removing stagnant orgone energy and gives visual movement of the energy center.

If the energy around a chakra is moving counterclockwise instead of clockwise, it can be interpreted as a disturbance in the physical, emotional or etheric level of a body field or if the chakra is completely still it can indicate the center is not open, fully blocked by condensed energy. Most likely dysfunction is related to a physical or emotional disturbance but definitely requires attention.

Wearing a piece of amethyst containing small amounts of iron around your neck assists in grounding your energy for focused reverence to the session.

Soothing music engineered with sounds that assist in balancing the centers can be very helpful and relaxing as well as crystal or Tibetan bowls. Begin at the feet using light pressure reflexology to check the energy flow in body systems. For example, eighty percent of people carry tension in their neck and back and compressing reflex points in that meridian improves energy flow. You can do this for yourself by pressing with your thumb on the instep part of the foot beginning at the heel and pressing as you go up the foot towards the base of the big toe. Continue to press with your thumb around the neck or base of the big toe. You may experience a tingling sensation in the spine which only serves to bring awareness of tension in that area but the overall result is relaxation. Once the person's body is calmed you can begin deep breathing and placing your hands on the soles of the feet or holding an ankle in each hand. If working on yourself when relaxed get into a comfortable position that you can totally let go of awareness of physical state. Place your hands on your body where you feel directed or comfortable.

While deep breathing with eyes closed repeat the person's name (or your own name if channeling for yourself) in your mind and with caring intention send it into the universal field.

Remember each one of us has a personal vibration that we are trying to reconnect to a universal energy source at these times of focus. When placing the person's name into the field you are in a sense recalibrating the frequency.

What I see as this is happening appears like a night sky filled with constellations and stars. It is a dark void filled with bright specks. Dark matter is living energy moving slower than the spectrum of light and constantly expands and contracts from vibrations in our universe resulting from super novae and black holes. Light and darkness are both living forms of energy that constantly move and we can affect that movement.

Once you reconnect with the person's vibration this whole star filled blackness begins to slowly swirl in a clockwise movement until a vortex is formed and energy flows downward entering through the crown chakra. The connection is made as energy flows and circulates through you and into the other person through the hands. At this point intentionally direct a vertical flow through the crown chakra straight down the spine and out through the root chakra into the earth. To ground oneself visualize deep roots of energy growing from the feet wrapping around ancient forest tree roots, continuing through deep layers of rock formations, underground pools of water and further into the center of the earth. Then allow grounding Earth energy to return up the roots and into your body. You now have energy flowing through the spine coming in from above and in from below. I see this as white streams of flowing energy cleansing blockages in the vertical center in order to receive and channel its flow. In one direction the white flow enters from above and travels down the spine exiting the root chakra but re-circulates in and out as a continuous circle around and around. The other direction of flow enters from below travelling up the spine and exits the crown chakra but again re- circulates in and around in a continuous circle.

When the vertical flow is completely cleared, bands of energy begin to enter through the fronts of chakras and exit through the backs of chakras again re-circulating in and out in a continuous motion. This action assists energy centers to straighten, open and move in a clockwise direction creating uninhibited flow.

The next clearing occurs in each chakra by visualizing the clarity of color and direction of movement beginning with the first or root chakra.

Visualize a red colored root chakra moving in a clockwise direction and wait until it is clear in color and movement before moving onto the second orange sacral chakra and so on until you reach the crown chakra. When you see all of the centers in bright, clear color and clockwise movement then energy begins to shoot upward from the front of all chakras and turns into bright white intense light filling your egg shaped field. In essence it looks like blowing and filling a balloon.

At this stage you are able to entrain with another person repeating the same process of clearing their chakras until their energy field is expanded. Intentionally direct the incoming flow of energy through the hands into a body to begin searching for physical, emotional, or mental imbalances that are creating disharmony.

I pray for Jesus to heal through me and visualize his hands on me as a vessel for his healing energy. A prayer or words can be anything that moves your spiritual vibration into a faster and higher frequency. Whatever your belief in a higher power is a helpful focus.

During the entire session the eyes are closed allowing high sense perception to guide with inner vision for information. Begin asking for what answers you need, for healing you require; then just let it flow and listen to what comes. There is great wisdom found in the space of stillness.

Trusting what you feel, or perceive comes with practice. Since we are beings wired into our solid world of static five senses to determine our surroundings, it is harder to have faith looking into our energetic subatomic world.

It is okay to seek confirmation for what you perceive particularly when working on another person. Energy comes to us in many forms including information and often the message or impression coming through may not make any sense to you but does for the person you are working with. When you are in a high sense perception state your awareness of the physical world is diminished and you read things differently. Many times I am directed to ask for assistance from others who have passed over and they may be present for that person's healing. When asking what is needed for this person you may be shown an area in their physical body requiring intense focus by placing your hands directly on the spot.

You may be shown past emotional events that you can bring attention and awareness to yielding immense release in that area of the person's field. I have felt deep seated repression in bodies from social beliefs or parental beliefs strongly influencing their life that created deep rifts or tears in energy fields. There is a lot of fear operating in people creating anxiety, depression, and unhappiness. Many times an entire session is spent holding a higher frequency of love and compassion for a soul who feels alone or disconnected.

Move from the feet and address each energy center beginning with the root chakra, next the sacral chakra and so on placing your hands about two inches above the body or directly on the body if needed, never leaving their field, and end at the head or crown chakra. When hands are placed on and around the head a comforting spiritual connection elicits great peace. Visualize an intense beam of white or blue light passing through your hands clearing the person's spine and exiting the root chakra.

This assists in removing tension or pain in the back and neck.

As the session comes to a close, ask for blessings for this soul as they travel on their human journey. Evoking a feeling of reverence when closing a session seals your intention; felt within the emotional layer of the person's field or heart chakra. Mist the essential oil chakra blend into your field and the other person's field and slowly step back until you feel the separation of the body fields.

Summarizing the Channeling Process

a. Take personal inventory of physical, emotional and mental states before channeling.

b. Find a relaxed position enabling a release of tension in all muscles while deeply breathing in through the nose and out through the mouth.

c. Choose a prayer or words created around love, truth, spirituality and healing that raise your vibration and visualize a white light surrounding you for protection from unwanted lower energy frequencies.

d. Close the eyes and focus only on breathing until you can begin to visualize a dark void filled with bright specs. Place a name or your own into the space as it begins to swirl and spiral downward connecting with the crown chakra.

e. Continue to allow the white energy to enter through the crown chakra flowing down the spine and exiting the root chakra in a re-circulating motion. Allow energy to flow in and out through the fronts and backs of all centers.

f. Visualize roots of energy growing from the feet into Mother Earth grounding you in solid foundation.

g. Begin at the root center visualizing a clockwise

clear red color movement.

h. Move up the spine to the next sacral center visualizing clockwise clear orange color movement and so on until reaching the crown chakra.

i. Visualize flowing energy from all centers filling your egg shaped energy field with intense healing white light.

j. Begin assessing physical areas and seeking answers for what is required for healing to take place.

k. Place your hands wherever you feel guided, feeling for intensifying heat on areas requiring balance. Pay attention to visual impressions, or messages presented.

l. Close the channel in a state of reverence and gratitude.

Following this guide can be helpful for invoking healing energy or preparing for a session to assist another. Intentions are crucial and this cannot be emphasized enough as karmic law prevails; what ye sow, so shall ye reap or do unto others as you would have them do unto you. Remaining open to everything but attached to nothing that is channeled is an important rule to follow.

After the trauma of losing Ryan and John's injury I fell into a low vibration unable to hold channeled energy at the level needed for healing and decided to cancel all appointments. I believe it is critical to take an honest inventory particularly when assuming responsibility for assisting others. I desperately wanted to help my brother, attempting a session; however I struggled to hold the frequency and was aware of a lesser healing intensity.
I did observe an immense hole above his heart chakra and the center was completely closed and inharmonious of its flow of energy in and out.

Understandably this confirmed his broken heart from losing Ryan. I urged him to seek help from professional sources and not to wait.

Healing energy is anything and everything and always present. It is bringing light where there is darkness, love where there is fear, compassion where there is anger and always grace and unity to the AT ONE MENT.

God is the One; we are part of the One and altogether our Oneness makes the whole.

We may not understand this other unseen world that influences who and what we are but brilliant people are diligently working with science to shed light on these mysteries. In time we may all come together seeing through the unawareness and for the first time as a world, be unified in truth and light.

Protection

Protecting ourselves against negative energies takes awareness of thoughts and feelings when encountering energy fields from people, places or environmental surroundings that make you feel unsettled, unwell, anxious or lethargic.

There are several ways of raising or inflating your energy field, but one of my favorites is using the Octahedron or Holon of balance. Imagine the shape of a pyramid seeing it clearly in your mind's eye; now imagine the shape of a pyramid turned upside down. Join the two bottoms of the pyramids together so that you have two tips where one is pointing up and the other down. Visualize yourself sitting or lying inside the pyramids in the middle where the two bottoms meet and the vertical line from the tips run right through you. Deeply breathe, relax, and visualize the inside of your octahedron filled with any color you desire.

If you practice this often enough it will become your sanctuary of peace and well-being.

Even if you are out and about and have encountered a negative experience you can sit in your parked car and take a few minutes visualizing and breathing inside your octahedron rebalancing and regrouping into a state of positive energy. It is like having a personal mind spa.

Octahedron

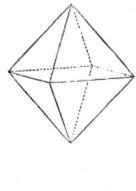

Geometry itself reveals spiritual concepts including its reference in the Bible. The circle represents the Godhead; all that was, is and ever shall be. It is in a state of perfect balance with no beginning or end; infinite. The triangle represents the trinity, Father-Son-Holy Ghost, father-mother-god, spirit-soul-mind, and the three levels super-conscious, subconscious, and conscious. In the two interlaced triangles of the Star of David, geometry captures the axiom, "As above, so below".

The upper triangle is the world of spirit, and the lower triangle is the world of matter. Geometry validates that we see only half the truth. That is why by placing yourself in the middle of the octahedron you are equally in the world of spirit and world of matter. You are in a place of complete balance as you receive energy from above at the top point and energy from below at the lower point. As you sit in the middle the points of energy align through your vertical center.

The mathematical truths reveal the angles of a triangle equal one hundred and eighty degrees and by adding the two triangles together we have three hundred and sixty degrees.

The angles of a square equal three hundred and sixty degrees and a circle also contains three hundred sixty degrees.

So we can say that a circle contains all truth and wisdom, a triangle gives us half the truth until joined. Symbolically we live in the lower half of the triangle; or the world of matter, so we must look to the spirit in the upper triangle to find the truth for completion. The square is symbolic of the earth, the four points on the compass, north, east, south, and west, the four elements of fire, earth, air, and water; the four points on the cross and the four points of body, mind, soul, and spirit. Our body belongs to the earth, but our soul belongs to the spirit.

"Love that shines from within cannot be darkened by obstacles of the world of consequences." ___ Pythagoras

"Only when your quiet mind is silent and listens and your heart is full of love – only then God talks with you."
___ Pythagoras

Pythagoras Divine Triangle Life Theorem blue print

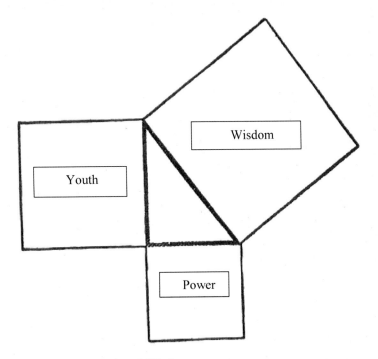

Figure 1 Youth, Power, and Wisdom

Pythagoras believed that numbers alongside the alphabet mapped out pathways of life. Each letter of an individual's name was represented by a number and could be added to birth dates to give insight into the human journey. He believed everything in the universe passed through progressive cycles and his measurement of cycles were the numbers 1 through 9. Every number over 9 reduces to one of these digits. Take the number of days in a year 365; add 3+6+5=14 and further reduced 1+4 =5. Each number carries a unique characteristic or esoteric quality. Number 5 as an example represents freedom, change and constant activity. Numbers represent universal principles of evolution and growth through cyclic sequence.

Every name vibrates to a number and every number has inner meaning. You were born on a certain date, hour and minute into the earth's energy field. The vibrations of the field at time of birth determine much that will characterize your life. The study of numbers evolved into the ancient science of **Numerology**, still in practice. The Divine Triangle is the basis of the Pythagorean Theorem, a blue print that can describe the magnitude of our lives. The blueprint is formed by the triangle of mind, soul and spirit added to the square of the physical body and matter. The triangle is the foundation on which the squares are built, each side of three lines representing nine years of life. The left square represents our youth from year one to age twenty seven. The lower square refers to our Power years from age twenty seven to fifty four and the upper square represents living through wisdom gained from life experience. It includes age fifty four to eighty one. After reaching age eighty one we begin the cycle once again from the youth square but on a higher vibration.

Numerology is yet another tool we can investigate for insight and knowledge. We all search for meaning to life pondering spiritual mystery and question why things happen to us. In numerology we can determine our Life Lesson number derived from the birthdate which represents things we must learn or overcome. This number carries influence on choices of career. We can determine our soul number which represents the real personality, the inner secret self, a number found from adding the vowels in the full name given at birth providing a deeper look into our real self. The outer personality number shows what others expect from you or how they see you by the image you present even though this projection is not what your inner self may be like. The number is found by adding the consonants in the full name at birth. The path of destiny number shows what you came to manifest in this life, what you must do.

It represents your aim, the path you walk to accomplish what you must be. This number will persist in its desire for expression throughout your life. The point is when we are feeling baffled and out of sorts numerology can help us to gain insight into why things in our lives unfold the way they do.

Tarot has been a reliable tool for insight when I have felt something is not right but cannot put my finger on the source of disharmony. If one can focus feelings and thoughts into a specific question Tarot gives amazing answers. Tarot is ancient and its origin is quite a mystery steeped in rich symbolism. Truth from this ancient wisdom has been taught by the Rosicrucians, Masons and includes symbols of alchemy and astrology. It has been suggested to be a symbolic alphabet of the Qabalah.

Interpreted symbols reflect the vibrational level you are on by revealing your present attitude towards life and conditions you must confront in present time. One or the other may be out of balance so change your attitude and you change your conditions or vice versa. Tarot can aid your perceptions about yourself opening doors to understand who you are where you are going and how you will get there. It can help to shed light on some confusing thoughts or decisions where you have to choose one or the other. Always by changing our thoughts we then affect our attitudes which change the outcome of any situation. Each symbol tells a story and the seventy eight cards weave many stories, always truthful and accurate. Tarot can be used for obtaining knowledge for understanding what is occurring in present time giving you control for making positive choices that lead to harmony within yourself. Tarot is used for drawing out the wisdom hidden in the heart of mankind. Symbolism of the lower arcana consisting of 56 cards represents planes of existence. Wands represent spirit, fire and Leo. Cups represent soul, water and Scorpio.

Swords represent man, air and Aquarius. Pentacles represent the natural world, earth and Taurus. Holding the cards while focusing on the question you seek an answer for imprints a vibration into the cards so that when a sequence of cards is read a thread of knowledge is woven providing an answer surrounding the situation at hand allowing one to make adjustments to attitude or change the conditions surrounding the situation. Books explaining how to use Tarot decks can be a valuable self- help tool. It is a much deeper subject to investigate if the brief introduction feels right for you.

Emotional Freedom Technique involves a very specific procedure whereby one identifies a negative issue by placing it in an affirmative statement to contradict the pattern. Example: **Even though I am _____ I deeply and completely accept myself.** While this statement is repeated out loud one taps meridian points near the surface of the body. When tapped these points interrupt the energy flow while the brain is focused on the thought at hand. EFT is a re-programming sequence of negative energy and can even help in reversing the polarity in the energy system. This is called Psychological Reversal because the imbalance can impede all areas of healing and performance. It is caused by self-defeating, self-sabotaging, negative thoughts, outside of your awareness in the subconscious mind and thwarts any attempts at healing physically or emotionally. Instead of experiencing positive emotions with acceptance those with psychological reversal experience them as uncomfortable and inadvertently undo them. If your subconscious mind is set on thwarting your success you will find it harder to attain and sustain positive change. Energies within become oriented to respond and sustain unhappiness rather than happiness. While most people find pleasure in healing therapy PR individuals have subconscious blocks to feeling happy.

Subconsciously they resist letting go of their emotional distress symptoms such as fears or depression. The reason is found in the body's energy system and reversing oneself allows the body's natural healing processes to work more at ease. The cause of all negative emotions is a disruption in the body's energy system.

The sequence: Use the index finger and tap lightly approximately seven times while repeating your affirmation. **I love and accept myself even though I have this** _____. Firstly tap with the dominant hand at the beginning of the brow just above and to one side of the nose, next on the bone bordering the outside corner of the eye, then on the bone under the eye below your pupil, next midway between the upper lip and under the nose, then midway between the point of your chin and lower lip, next the junction where the breast bone and collarbone and first rib meet then on the side of the body about four inches below the arm pit. Another helpful place is located on the sub clavicles located on the chest midway above the breast. On these two spots rubbing in a circular motion while repeating your affirmation is also useful for upsetting psychological reversal. EFT can be used on any negative thought and as many times during a day as necessary. Of course this is an over simplified explanation of EFT but again most importantly you can use this technique to bring relief and rid yourself of negative emotional burdens that have interrupted happiness even perhaps since childhood. If EFT makes sense then I would recommend further investigation into the theory and technique as it has truly helped many and can be added to the tool chest of self-help.

Harmonizing Mind and Body

We must recognize the importance of harmonizing the mind with the body. Stress and excessive thinking are hazardous to our health. As Eckhart Tolle eloquently explained, when we harmonize the mind with the body in the present moment, something profound happens. Stress and worry begins to transcend, the body relaxes, and energy flows uninhibited, resulting in wellness and inner joy. Deepak Chopra speaks of inner awareness as a means to stop looking in our external world for contentment by placing attention to what is happening in our inner world.

By taking inventory of how the inner self is feeling physically and mentally at any given moment we become free of worry and thoughts of the future and the past in our outer world. Inner awareness combined with a relaxed state allows energy to flow easily, healing our body and opening our mind to all possibilities.

Praying or meditating increases the speed of our vibration and raises us to a higher frequency of energy flow in our body field. Hence we hear the statement, contentment and happiness comes from within. There is no one person or thing that can "make" us happy. Taking responsibility and accepting that personal happiness is between you and a higher power elicits inner peace that radiates outward from your energy field to those around you. You share happiness with others by positive energy flowing into their fields of energy.

Having an earthly physical life is such an honor. We can choose to live in joy and explore our world of greatness seeing its splendor and mysteries or wallow in despair and negativity seeing only limiting walls.

As Buddha taught, life is of suffering that we must first understand before we can appreciate joy.

Grieving is Unworldly

Tragedies affecting families bringing unfathomable grief and despair may not resonate and create the same reaction in others. Even within the family each person's response may vary due to Karmic understanding from past experience woven into their soul fabric already.

My pain and suffering resulting from personal tragedy cannot be completely absorbed into the psyche of another unless a similar experience has been shared. This is just the way of it. We think we can empathize in understanding but truly we cannot. That is why we must never sit in judgment of each other, for what is real and unfolding into all my senses may not be part of your reality. Let us give one another compassion during times in our personal journeys that rob us of joy. Love and kindness are earthly gifts to share with each other, for what my lessons are teaching me in this lifetime you may experience in your next life. An offering of patience and non-interference is most often a gesture of kindness.

Tragedies may scar us emotionally and test our beliefs, but surviving the experience through an open heart profoundly affects how we reunite with our soul's purpose.

Grieving is a process unlike no other human experience.

It is a time we turn inward to deal with incredible imbalances occurring in our mental, emotional and physical bodies. There is little in the external world that can help us including professional and familial networks. One becomes so inwardly absorbed in the state of dysfunction and pain that eating, sleeping, working, walking, talking all seem impaired. It is a rare chance we get to be closer to our soul's essence and spiritual support because at this level we are disconnected from our physical personalities.

In a zombie- like state we wander aimlessly trying to find help from anyone or anything to ease our suffering but in the end it comes down to that place within ourselves that we reconcile and accept the information our grief has brought into existence.

While grieving for Ryan and John I relented completely and unabashedly to despair and sadness in the moments when I was overwhelmed. Although my mind desired to escape to a place in the past or a place in the future I gave myself over to healing in the present moment each time an emotion was aroused. Remaining fully present in thought and emotion instead of escaping to a zone of comfort is a monumental task during times we grieve. Our bodies respond in reactions of trembling, nausea, crippling muscle pain, debilitating headaches and at times hyperventilating into panic attacks at the mere thought of leaving the home.

Indeed we may feel our body and mind deceive us as disconnected entities re-cycling chaos in dizzying proportions. Focusing on faith and a higher power when we are in a weakened state and having a mantra to repeat each time you feel overwhelmed such as... **This too shall pass**...are necessary staples.

I lovingly allowed myself to release freely when I needed to discharge pent up energy. Some become uncomfortable seeing others in emotional distress and often jump in with intentions to soothe when in fact it may prevent the person from releasing negative energy.

Usually a silent comforting hug is all a person needs to feel embraced in compassion. There is no time limit on grieving and it manifests in several ways other than emotional.

Previous problems deserve little concern or energy as focus changes course on priority and importance of needs and wants. Favorite foods, pastimes, patterns of sleep, entertainment, hobbies, fashion choices and friends may change during times of grief.

Our five senses are out of whack interpreting our physical world as if we are in a dreamlike trance.

Patience and unconditional acceptance of our thoughts and feelings by us and others along with no forced commitments or demands is the best prescription for healing through this state. Time may not heal us completely but eventually we do calm down to a place of acceptance.

Healing in the Present Moment

The verb "Heal" comes from the Anglo – Saxon word "haelan" which means to make whole. Mind, body, and spirit must be healed as one and "made whole" with thoughtful consideration given to each component.

When aware of yourself internally and externally using your five senses you are fully present in the physical world. When we fully understand the concept of living in the moment we feel free in our thinking and feelings and can initiate Healing in the present Moment. The moment we are living presently, this very minute, is the only thing we know for certain. We cannot heal a past hurtful experience unless we re-live the feelings and thoughts in this present moment where we can either change our attitude or change the condition around that particular experience in order for healing in the present moment to occur, right now, at this minute in time. You must be able to live and breathe the bad memory re-connecting the thought pattern about the memory that plagued you along with the emotions you felt at the time bad experience occurred as well as physical sensations felt in the body. Right now, at this moment in time you have the power to change whatever you desire with internal information, (thoughts and feelings), and heal yourself in that present moment from a troubling past experience. It may take a number of attempts but from good detective work one can gain freedom by giving new information to the negative occurrence or by accepting or making peace with the experience. We can heal in the present moment and return to the inherent state of zestful intelligence. As I type these words I have no assurance, control or responsibility for what will take place in life one hour from now or one month from now. As I sit in peace at this moment in one hour disruption from several directions could take place but why feel anxious for what has not occurred?

The experiences of yesterday have been assimilated so why worry about what has been? We can take responsibility for our actions and make corrections where needed but dwelling on what is past or will be drains life energy unnecessarily.

Taking physical inventory during the day can stop the mind from racing to anxiety by using an internal checklist. Ask yourself, how am I feeling right now? Are my muscles tense or relaxed? Am I breathing slow and deep or rapid and shallow? Is there pain in my body? Are my thoughts worried and angry or peaceful and happy? During the moment of inventory if there are no reasons for feeling stressed allow yourself to feel blessed.

The goal of total awareness and complete rationality is common among us and each gain in rationality brings enjoyment to life. Relationships with other people become more enjoyable and awareness of our surroundings increases our enjoyment of places and things when we are in a rational state. When we encounter stress we have built in mechanisms that help us repair damage and if they are allowed to operate normally we are restored to intelligent function. They are identified as crying, trembling, and anger discharge, yawning and laughing. If we are allowed and supported during the healing process by a person who is truly present and does not interfere or distract us we usually release the hurt and then move on to our normal life.

Healing within all levels of the human field occurs rapidly once a traumatic emotional disturbance has been dealt with first and in fact more commonly the long standing emotional dis-ease had manifested into physical dis-ease. Beliefs in our body's ability to heal are established at a very early age in life. If our parents had us believe the only way to get well came from a visit to the doctor you would probably refer to that your whole life. The mind sending messages of how to heal is extremely potent.

Most of us learned how to clean and bandage wounds on the body at an early age but skills to heal emotional wounds were mostly non-existent in childhood years.

It is common that people have disconnected from the magnificent intelligence and power within our bodies. Another road block to healing comes from fear patterns affecting choices made in daily living and these can be as diverse as the imagination will allow but cannot be discredited. Our fear based beliefs hinder us from seeing the truths of a loving universe.

We continually seek others to be aware listeners even though most times it is non-fulfilling. We are left to wonder what it would feel like to have someone really, deeply interested in us and it seems most commonly, our most bitter disappointment is that our loved ones do not listen or are not interested in hearing our deeply felt concerns and wishes.

We all feel this need for someone to give us authentic attention, really listen to us and compassionately care about us and we never really give up trying to get our hurts out of our system. The problem is we have been conditioned from childhood to control our repair mechanisms by such comments as "there now it's okay, don't cry" or "get a grip on yourself" or "shut up" or "Please stop crying, you are making me feel bad" or the best of all tactics is distraction, interruption or redirecting to another subject.

For example when a child is happy and laughing those around will not interfere but if the child is crying or angry, adults rush in to stop the "negative" behavior. Children usually express themselves in uninhibited abandonment until others step in to stop the release of negative emotion which causes them to choke back their feelings. If allowed to release their feelings, in a short while the experience usually ends with a sigh, yawn or smile and they move on to another activity.

If they are inhibited during their release then the upset becomes an unfinished, unresolved, confused emotion that is stored as a distress memory that may replay in similar response throughout life. The interference in a person releasing distresses can cause them to stuff or suppress the uncomfortable outcome of the experience. It is then heaped onto the pile of accumulated and unresolved hurt issues that may form distress patterns which determine our future response actions. As we grow older we gain wisdom and coping skills through life experience to better understand human emotions but many unresolved issues from childhood follow us.

The aftermath following emotional turmoil eventually brings calm after the storm. I believe we are given these restful times in order for us to digest and assimilate what a particular experience brought to us. Reflection leads to deciphering emotions from reactions and mental concepts that we believe to be true. Our experiences give us a data base for reference when we encounter similar future incidents. They develop into old patterns that we rely on for immediate response without much thought or energy. These reliable old patterns of reaction allow us to drift unconsciously. Thank goodness we now understand that drifting on automatic pilot is not in our best interest and through awareness we begin to recognize the power to change our reactions.

There are times in life we become stuck in mental and emotional circles of unresolved painful and negative issues. These issues form chronic patterns that return to hurt us over and over each time there is a familiar trigger.

Until we are able to revisit the mis-stored information of the chronic pattern through conscious intention for connecting the emotion to our thoughts, staying fully aware of the two throughout the reconnection process, we cannot unravel the painful past experience.

By being aware of our thoughts at any given moment we

can challenge old patterns, bringing desired change by giving our experience new information, ensuring future reactions will be different and healthier.

Re-evaluation of thoughts and emotions from a negative encounter allows healing in the present moment to occur; as truth heals incorrectly interpreted mental thoughts and emotions. Healing is confirmed and revealed in body language as zestful, lighter, more energetic and relaxed. The recovery process is confused memory of bad experience freed by emotional release that is evaluated and converted into ordinary information.

It is the moment we remark Aha! or Oh, now I see!

It is necessary to have an intimate conversation with oneself as healing in the present moment requires honesty in personal inventory of thought, emotion, and physical symptom but remember self-criticism and self-judgment enhances destructive thoughts that lead to feelings of inadequacy and guilt creating an inability to sympathize with ourselves. The direction of self-approval is more dependable in resolving chronic patterns as this is the most common area of distress. Expressions of affection contradict every hurt stored within us. To completely appreciate and love our self is the ultimate direction from irrationality.

Healing in the present moment allows us to break down the negative experience we find ourselves in by asking questions such as, what is making me sad? What has triggered my emotions? What is the source; a person, their words, an incident or a hurtful memory? In the moment of considering our response we re-visit the details, examining each question until we identify the nature of the emotion. In the moment of awareness when re-evaluating details of information from an experience, allow yourself to bring the feeling into present time while aware of what your thoughts about the feeling reveal and ask yourself questions.

Did this really happen, is this truthful, is this still relevant in present time or is this a past memory that no longer requires the same response, can I change the situation, can I make amends, can I accept or forgive, can I release the hurt, can I have a different attitude now that I understand why I carried this negativity with me for so long? Healing begins by acknowledging what happened in the past is done, that moment will never occur again to hurt us the same way. The past serves to remind us that we can do things differently when creating each new day. We are free and only responsible for how we choose to live today and how we respond to problems that arise today. Each time you find yourself overwhelmed in moments of sorting internal dialogue, take a deep breath and visualize yourself as an expanded orb of powerful energy sending away the negative suffering to the universe.

Deeply breathe in peace and let yourself feel problems and tension dissolving as you imagine living in a universe that creates loving peaceful bliss. Feel gratitude in your heart for the goodness you receive and enjoy the gift of harmony as you bathe in spiritual love.

Healing in the present moment takes awareness, willingness and determination for a desired change within and without to occur. When we understand the evolution of our emotional and mental growth and how it influences our lives we become free to make new responses.

Core energetics is a unified process of inner healing which concentrates on working through the ego and personality to unblock energies in the body. If you continue to judge yourself the results will mirror the expression of actions and feelings reflecting your judgments.

One needs to be aware of thoughts to discover where one might be blocking energy flow; distanced from the control of ego and letting our soul's intelligence guide us. What we desire to bring into existence will define our intention to fulfill our needs.

199

"Be careful of your thoughts for thoughts become your words. Be careful of your words for words become your actions. Be careful of your actions for actions become your habits. Be careful of your habits for habits become your character. Be careful of your character for that becomes your destiny. "___Dwight

Live Gently

North American society sets out to unify its people by herding them into timely schedules beginning in childhood. We presume that waking at a given hour each day is a healthy practice. We set our alarm clocks (notice the word "alarm") jolting our consciousness to offending noise. Before our brain has a chance to focus we assault our bodies by pouring hot stimulants down our throat just so we can see our way to the shower. We trundle off following predetermined schedules deemed efficient for managing organized society. Does it?

We are forced to work and learn on days and times that may not coincide with our own biological needs creating stress upon our physical and emotional states of health. We eat according to schedules, not when our bodies need sustenance.

We impatiently count down the last minutes of work just to hurry up and wait in rush hour traffic lamenting unanimously, just let me get home.

Our evenings are filled with cooking, homework, and chores until we wearily fall into bed, setting the alarm for the routine to begin all over again.

So I wonder why it is we continue this mainstream madness until we become worn out and weary adults.

Our world seems structured on multi-level will and ego. We have lost rather than gained civility amongst ourselves under the name of correctness as we struggle to redefine our roles as female and male and global unification.

How inane and ludicrous to enlightened minds that under the appellation of religion people are enslaved, beaten and robbed of human dignity and liberty.

What an insult to mankind and God to witness fanatical religious will power stealing away people's freedom by martialed conformity.

It is inconceivable that even today a belief that God

chooses to love one race or religion over the other remains in circulation. There is only one creator, the rest is just genetics and even atheists concede to a belief in a creative force.

Will power and self-centered ego continue to fuel the ever burning need to be right. How utterly ridiculous to entertain that type of thinking, yet here we are in the twenty first century stuck in our squabble of ancient misinterpreted and misunderstood ideals that still influence the all-consuming need for domination.

Fear is created when there is lack of truth and love. Instead of improving the lives of ourselves, neighbors, friends and family, we collectively continue creating unrest.

We have lost kindness, patience and good manners when interacting socially, compassionate health care, and protection of the vulnerable members of our society such as the elderly and innocent children. We need to take a deep breath, pause, and feel what lies in our heart before we leap.

Mankind's spirituality developed in isolation within nations over centuries as geographically we were separated. Now that we are globally connected "sabers are rattled" as cultures cling to historical religious practices. It is human nature, because ego and will power is to be human, that our beliefs are correct, therefore the struggle for spiritual unity without doctrine and simply agreeing upon a creative force will take time.

Prophecy claims we are entering into a "New Age" of consciousness; perhaps this is brought about by external circumstances that force us to look upon life and existence together in a different light.

Due to an external physical shift enlightenment may dawn in conscious thought creating beliefs founded in truth, love and all-knowing intelligence as we see our place in the world clearly defined.

The time is coming that simply existing by using our five

senses will not be sufficient.

The sooner people open their minds and hearts to understanding we create life by the connection to our invisible world, the sooner we can bring unity from chaos. What I have come to understand through different sessions of channeling is that old ways of thinking, particularly from controlling male energy, will dissolve as realization dawns we are two spiritual halves melding in wholeness of masculine and feminine energy and in time eliminate power struggles politically, financially and personally.

Religious leaders power over their followers will weaken as truth emerges into consciousness that mankind can heal by the piece of God within each soul.

Peace felt through the heart that no man or woman has superiority over another, will dissolve powers of ego that falsely rule the earth.

In fact, those living in humility and joyful compassion will emerge as pillars of strength showing the masses a new direction for living gently upon Mother Earth in harmony, love and peace, foretold to reign for a thousand years.

Life upon the earth will change, we already know this. How will you prepare? Who am I? (I AM), Why am I here? (I AM). Is God (I AM) within me?

Look into your life for what needs to be healed emotionally, turning your heart towards God (IAM) for the answers you seek for there you will find your truth and manifest healing. Move the focus of living life from mental decisions into the heart where you feel what should be done instead of leaving it in thought.

It is through your heart that you have the greatest connection to the universal field. It is no wonder heart disease has escalated to one of the highest causes of death as we have been closed and disconnected to our feelings far too long. Remember metaphysically speaking, Louise Hay defines "heart problems as serious long standing emotional problems where there is lack of joy and rejection to life."

We have lived in emotional dysfunction within society and even our own families. When people relate their concerns, they have no problem verbalizing thoughts, but when asked what they are feeling become stuck and immediately struggle to find an answer. Feelings intuitively guide us bringing balance to the ever active mind where often words fail to give full explanation. Words cannot replace a deeply felt emotion looking for expression.

We have manifested an imbalance between our thinking and feelings creating more discord and apathy towards one another. One only needs to view a news cast or read a newspaper to find daily examples of this behavior. We have lost the feeling of living gently within our families, communities, cities, and world.

There is a great deal of intolerance rising in waves of impatience. Does it really matter if the person in front of the line is counting out small change?

Is it worth getting into an accident driving recklessly because you may be three minutes late for your appointment? If you are angry that everyone moves too slowly, poor you.

If you could take an inventory of your body physically reacting to your emotions you would feel its response is the same as if you were a warrior fighting a battle for your life. As my Dad would say, "If you are in that much of a hurry, you should have left a little sooner."

You can think of hundreds of examples taken from conversations around you from stressed individuals who are bursting at the seams with anxiety. This all revolves around time as we are adjusting through the shift in our cosmic and physical world, time is sped up and we cannot possibly fit in all that we used to within our familiar concept of time.

Stop jamming so many things into one day; you're just going to make yourself ill if you don't start prioritizing soon. At the end of your days are your memories of life going to be about work, or vacations, people or things? Will you remember your joy of meditating beneath the blossoming apple tree on a spring day, or the hectic commute fretting lateness?

Is your memory of joy sharing thanksgiving with family and friends stronger than working through the holiday to impress your boss? They sound like logical easy to answer questions but many fall into a structured routine and do not prioritize important issues until it is too late.

Even if you have not made the conscious connection yet, somewhere inside you know that change is coming, we all do. Put your time where it means the most for you and your loved ones.

Love, true love only comes knocking at your door once maybe twice in a lifetime. Unconditionally loving another and feeling reciprocated love is a key element which profoundly affects our quality of life. A common regret recounted from elderly persons is of a lost unrequited love from youth that was never found again in the remainder of their life. During mid-life or late life true love is wonderful, fulfilling, unhurried, and gentle. Basking in its perfection is all too short as years pass quickly and health declines forcing goodbyes to the deep connection with our soul mate, leaving us to wonder how to carry on without them. Much ill-spent energy engaged in superficial drivel produces regret and wishes for a slower paced life to absorb the beauty and depth of emotion in the present moments shared with those we love.

That infinite connection of love felt in every cell of your being for another is immensely powerful, perfect. To leave this earthly life not knowing the feeling of love is sorrowful as it is the most basic gift given to humans yet ego and will has the power to deceive the heart.

205

Sabbatical

Everyone needs to take a break from a hectic routine now and again. We were fortunate to have a long vacation on the island of Roatan, Honduras and enjoyed a sabbatical from news and television.

Nature is raw and in control in breathtaking splendor on land and sea. Snorkeling pristine bays and reefs was other worldly and humbling if not intimidating seeing so much life and creation. Walking through lush verdant forests of abundant life in sync and perfect order was witness to miraculous evolution as creatures of every shape and size survive in harmony. Life hummed in simple balance for people in vibrant tones and color.

We stayed at Oceano Village secluded from night light and noise pollution bathed in natural beauty yet luxurious accommodation. We sat in peaceful bliss on our veranda gazing at the oceans horizon rising and falling as parrots chattered and sea birds glided gracefully above the mantas ballet in the lagoon below.

The night skies seem lower, every inch filled with stars blanketing earth as ocean breezes cool the land in comforting wisps.

Billowing clouds burst into showers of sun warmed rain during the day promoting a rain dance of happy, boisterous frogs at night.

Quaint villages mixed with developing tourism made me question how we keep the balance. We humans create beauty through structure yet strongly desire the purity of nature's gifts.

There was much opportunity for healing in the present moment through uninterrupted silence and meditation, fully aware and deeply grateful for the gift.

The Shift

Much has been prophesized for this period of mankind's evolution and the message is clear that apocalyptic (a prophetic revelation) change will occur as a new age has been foreseen to dawn. Awareness is needed and significant consideration given to thoughts mankind creates in the world during this time. If our minds carry thoughts of destruction through fear and war we have the collective power to manifest an end to life as we know it. If our hearts are creating thoughts and deeds of love and hope for peace to reign, then we have the collective power to manifest a new era of enlightenment, co-creating our existence with heaven and earth. Therefore all that has been written and foretold is a clear warning for us to heed that we have the power to create worldwide reality collectively for mankind by feelings and thoughts leading to potent actions.

Messengers from the oracles of light serving as teachers for mankind, herald the golden age as one of peace and unconditional love, foretelling this period to be a transition of mankind's consciousness. Some have chosen to prepare for this time of unfolding prophecy to aid during the changes upon the earth and in the hearts of man. Economic fluctuations will immobilize economies for the purpose of moving to one standard of trade and currency. We will see shifting and tumbling of world borders and political parties creating change in world leadership, but spiritual leaders will show the way during these troubled times. Each one of us must prepare our mind and heart for great change in order to identify truth, hope, and love when you learn, see and feel the harmony it creates in life. Replace fear by trust in the divine and courage in vision to call upon the heavenly spheres for aid in this dimension.

Woven Cloth

In moments of remembering I see how events and experiences were woven into a fabric of life, one strand beside the other. Every experience laid a foundation for the next one to occur and build on. One is unable to see this is happening in youthful years but slowly in time you become aware during moments of introspection that like weaving, one strand of thread lies beside or underneath another strengthening the fabric as does year after year of life. Nothing we ever do or learn is wasted, no matter its trivial nature. I sit in wonderment reflecting the perfection, in awe of invisible hands that set events in motion when I thought all along it was me in control.

My parent's tumultuous marriage provided the perfect environment needed for growth during this lifetime.

I absorbed from each of their character information that influenced my life, deciphering what was important or irrelevant.

I respected the unconditional acceptance and support by Dad who was warm hearted, humorous and enjoyed simple pleasures life brought. I felt sorrow that he worried and wasted precious time and energy on the smaller problems in life.

I respected the bottomless well of passion for life mother displayed, determined to make every occasion special and festive. Her attachment to the material world and disinterest in the spiritual world brought many challenges in my youthful years. Much later, I now look lovingly at mother with understanding that introspection was not part of her journey in this lifetime. I am grateful for the opportunities for inner growth she gave and enjoy the last days of our journey together.

Growing up in a land of lush flora and fauna nurtured my soul and enriched childhood in solid foundation.

Although it has taken many years while living in Alberta

to reconcile longings I now have come to love this beautiful land. I can even say I enjoy the calm and peace that come in the shorter, colder days of winter. Nature wastes no time in warmer months abundantly producing during the shorter growth cycle. Summers are lovely and the prairie skies are glorious. I am grateful that destiny brought me to this wonderful country, Canada.

Impressions from exposure to alcohol during childhood gave reference points for what showed up in my two marriages with Keith and John both having addictions to alcohol. Sensitivity and intuition as a child contributed to developed perceptive skills when gaging people and situations throughout adolescent years.

When I met Keith at age sixteen, he was a warm and sensitive young man who had his heart broken as his Mother left the family when he turned thirteen. Keith took the role of friend assisting his father to mend his bruised pride and bitter heart from divorce. Keith was lonely, and sought out friendships to fill the emotional void from his own sadness. Initially he displayed awkward social skills but soon found a side of his personality that attracted the attention he needed. He was generous and helpful to many that were in his circle of friends.

He failed miserably in roles of husband and father and as time went on became more and more disconnected from his soul. His choice to immerse himself in the physical world disregarding any spiritual, emotional dogma dominated his life.

I needed to learn from this relationship I could not change Keith's pathway of self-destruction no matter how hard I tried to rescue him. Instead, for me, it became a lesson of survival and self-preservation.

My brother and I have shared much together in life. We have always been there for each other through the highs and lows, laughing and crying, through prosperity and adversity.

Since childhood we have looked after each other whether throwing rotten apples across the creek at neighborhood bullies or holding each other up when we fall down in our darkest moments. We are different, yet the same by the blood of our parents and shared knowledge flowing within us. Two children surviving dysfunction and adversity took our place in the world always knowing we could depend on the other in times of need. I see the gentle humanitarian soul through the personality and I know he sees me. I am grateful I came into this world having him as my big brother.

Insight into the purpose of life on earth by serving others through love and compassion was a gift taught by Jesus. If we stop trying to help others that pass in and out of our lives then life becomes dull and barren. "You must learn to give before you can receive." These words were not written without purpose and guidance.

Each one of us that is a mother or father will go through the painful process of letting go of our children physically and emotionally as they continue to grow in their relationships with others. The emotional bonds severed over time leave twinges of sadness in your heart but this is the normal cycle of life. Understanding we lose importance in their lives is okay and in time will bring reverence as you enjoy the sacred cycle and joys of new life as grandchildren enter. For us and our children it makes letting go of our parents easier in the end of days. The bird that flies in freedom sings the sweetest. I realized I had to get out of Kimberlee's way so she could create her own cause and effect experiences to fulfill her destiny and purpose.

We must all come to terms with our partnered relationships; the ones we have chosen to let into our hearts. Feelings for each other will be tested in many ways and weather many emotional storms.

I learned that by choosing to love you must give and

receive unconditionally with your heart. Forgiveness may be the greater of our challenges, but there is no future without it.

There is much dissension and divorce as we struggle to identify and express our needs and feelings for one another. We rationalize, quarrel and counsel over material possessions instead of admitting the emotions creating the problems in the first place.

I observed the struggles John had throughout the years of his relationship with mother. In the early days he chose not to commit himself completely, wandering through emotions and personal dreams. His hesitance was due to their age difference and how it would affect his future. Instead of participating with creative choices he drifted through life finding decision making his biggest obstacle and now feels trapped and judged. I feel compassion for him as he struggles internally at this time.

As mother continues to drift away in the entanglement of her mind, sadly, she feels she was not able to find a man who loved her enough to marry. There is no rationalizing with her to understand John has been with her forty years because he loved her. I find myself wondering about the physical laws of life once again dictating our emotional life; could a marriage certificate really have changed her perception of love and happiness?

Witnessing dementia distort the person you have known and loved your entire life seems a cruel ending to Twilight years. The choice to be involved in caregiving until you no longer can or allow professional help to intervene is heart wrenching under any circumstance and should be a shared decision. Personally I do not want to be robbed of a single moment of clarity, or laughter from shared memories and find the more interaction we create, even if it takes great effort, the greater the rewards of unlocking treasures still in the mind.

The loss of loved ones leaves a space in our hearts and minds partly filled with memory, partly filled with regret. Each and every day they are missed and the heart aches in longing. Does time really heal tragic loss?

To say yes does not feel correct, how can we fully heal knowing we will never share our life with them again.

I think we learn in time not to dwell on our thoughts and feelings of the painful past, accepting what is, but we cannot deny the "if only" swelling our hearts in moments we remember. No matter the circumstance of how they left this world, they were knitted into our fabric of happiness and were once loved as innocent children by fathers and mothers.

Recently while in Honduras I was lucidly dreaming seeing Ryan and my father laughing and joking with each other. I felt the need to wake up and noticed it was the usual three fifteen A.M. I felt compelled to go out on the terrace and stood awestruck at the beauty of a million bright stars and one very luminous star slowly descending over the horizon. I stared, eyes filling with tears receiving the message. At Ryan's memorial it was said he was a brightly burning candle in life but was now a brightly burning star in heaven.

Our family dinners will never be the same, the seat will always be empty as we remember his laughter and spirit.

Dan will miss his son forever.

Each day I look at John I am filled with love and gratitude and at times emotionally overwhelmed. He continues to be a miracle getting stronger each and every day.

Addiction is no longer part of our life.

I know fully within my heart I witnessed divine intervention in John's healing. Our joy in life is in time we spend together. When apart we feel an uncomfortable absence in our hearts. Simple pleasures of everyday life, meet our needs. Material treasures have lost their gleam and attraction.

We both feel we have all we need and are immensely blessed to be together. We have a mutual understanding and a sense of knowing there is much more to life than what meets the eye.

Alcohol addiction can be treated through natural methods that do not further burden the physical field of the body.

Through nature's medicine chest we find herbs to calm the mind and body, herbs to detox inner organs, tissues and blood, and herbs to rebuild and support the rapid inner changes. Fomentations on the spine, liver, spleen, stomach and pancreas along with hot and cold water therapy, massage and reflexology are part of a natural therapy program that yields great success as well as nutritious, unprocessed, chemical free foods to speed up the recovery process. Most important are the energetic healing sessions that clear the layers of the human field. Emotional and mental wounds heal beautifully when reconnection with mind body and spirit is realized. The alcoholic personality is like the Emperor's new clothes, an illusion created to fulfill a souls desire to learn a chosen lesson through experience. Optimally a center for assisting those who want to end addiction through natural healing methods for the body, mind and spirit should exist.

To speak openly of the human experience sheds light into dark closets we seek to hide realities of life.

Media thrives on scandalous secrets and human misery for entertainment, fuelling shallow temptations for judgments however most often those that speak the loudest of condemnation have the most to hide. The world judged Ryan without truth and fact.

By remembering that for most of life we are only truly responsible for ourselves through our choices and actions, we are freed from the weight of responsibility and worry for what family, friends and humanity create. Can we turn attention towards enlightenment and healing adversities brought into existence, rather than sensationalizing the drama and vulnerabilities of being human?

Since the beginning humans have found ways of communicating important events whether it was gesture, illustration or word. Some cultures would sit in circles while a member would tell stories of his or her life that were meaningful in order for their memory to pass on to future generations. Many times these stories became plays acted out for younger children to remember their ancestors. Today we share these stories with family and friends through verbal or written word with subliminal messages, don't forget me. We share stories with hope that what we have learned through experience may inspire or provide knowledge for someone who may encounter a similar involvement. Word is our most powerful means of communicating, a form of expressing our inner most wishes and components of our personality, the essence of who we are.

Feeling guided to write the story, I can only assume it is part of my destiny unfolding; no different from life stories we each have come to manifest here on earth.

It is a reminder we will all have joy and sadness that shape who we are albeit free thinkers to choose creatively the direction our lives flow.

I have learned that in the darkest hours when I thought God had forgotten his promise never to bring more than I can handle; if I can but remember in the moments of horror and grief, that all I need to do is ask; a presence is soon there to fill me with strength and grace to get through.

We are given free will to "Ask and it shall be given you; seek and you shall find; knock and it shall be opened unto you (Matthew7:7) for Gods healing energy.

The place for focus is within yourself; here is where you begin your path of discovery, opening mind and heart to all possibilities and manifesting powerful energy into the physical, mental, and emotional bodies for well-being.

Spiritual love is and always has been within you and around you in abundance. All you need to do is awaken and recognize this beautiful gift. An awakened heart feels intuitive direction for living life for the greater good and senses right or wrong by vibrations sent throughout the body. Compassion and kindness influence decisions made from the heart and combined with rational thought guide us to live in balance.

Healing from trials in this journey of life must include with no exception forgiveness for wrong doings of others and mistakes we ourselves have made and will continue to make.

Healing must include compassion for others and self to replace fear by accepting imperfections through states of love and kindness.

Healing must include gratitude felt wholly within our being for all that we have and will have. Each breath, each day that is life should evoke gratitude.

Healing must include spirituality, a belief in a supreme power that rules the Universe for good.

Benjamin Franklin stood on a hill during a thunder storm inspired by nature's mighty power of lightning and set upon his quest to harness energy from "the heavens" to bring light into our world. From the beginning we have been captivated by nature's power of light as a source of God energy, so is it too far a reach to believe that we are in fact energetic beings that glow as bright light when we are not incarnated into three dimensional bodies?

Is there some inherent quality within us that inspires our search for bright stars as a familiar light we return to afterlife? We feel wonderment when people share their experience of returning to heaven through a tunnel of bright light expressed as loving and blissful.

In our language, we refer to ascension of consciousness as enlightenment or "seeing the light."

215

There are two ways of spreading light: to be the candle or the mirror that reflects it.

                          ___ Edith Wharton

A "dream" gave explanation to my constant search for understanding the term time – space – continuum. It was related to only a small percent of our genetic code is decoded with much awaiting discovery. The explanation given was; humans have a gene that is triggered near our time of death that prepares us to transcend a time space dimension to which we travel in a new state of matter, no longer requiring a physical body. Body matter is an illusion of our true source that can manifest into many forms.

Re-incarnation simply means we re-create another illusion, a new body that we reside temporarily. We then create a new illusionary life form in another dimension after earthly death and that is why we hear of near death experiences, being in heaven with former family.

Heaven is a different vision for each person yet part of a whole energetic creation. This one special gene is a gift of eternal life.

When preparing to leave a body the energy, spirit, rises upward from the root chakra towards the crown chakra. The root chakra is strong and vibrant through our teens; twenties and thirties as we are anchored in earthly life but weakens with age as our soul slowly rises closer to our spiritual center. An elderly wise minded person will show a weak root but strong crown center.

As we prepare to leave our body firstly the toes and feet curl, then heat gathers in the torso flushing the skin with redness as the energy or spirit prepares to exit and moments before death the eyes glow from energy that has ascended the body into the inner sanctum, an inner cavity located in the skull behind the forehead near the pineal gland that the soul ascends towards and into, in preparation for leaving the physical form.

All living things are part of a huge energy grid that we each send sparks through ever connecting pathways over and over for infinity.

My understanding is; the soul returns to heaven; and heaven is the sum of all of us, a mandala of souls, which joins with the creating energy source we call God.

Say not, "I have found the truth," but rather, "I have found a truth." Say not, "I have found the path of my soul."
Say rather, "I have met the soul walking upon my path," for the soul walks upon all paths. The soul walks not upon a line, neither does it grow like a reed. The soul unfolds itself, like a lotus of countless petals.

____ Khalil Gibran

The Lord will guide you always; he will satisfy your needs in a sun scorched land and will strengthen your frame. You will be like a well-watered garden, like a spring whose waters never fail.

____Isaiah 58:11

Oh Lord, you have made known to me the path of life; you will fill me with joy in your presence, with eternal pleasures at your right hand.

____Psalm 16:11

We fix our eyes on not what is seen, but what is unseen, for what is seen is temporary, but what is unseen is eternal.

____ Corinthians 4:18

My cup is full. I am grateful. I am blessed. I am loved and I love. I live joyfully. I let go and let live. I live gently and I am nourished. I Am.

Swiftly arose and spread around me the peace and
knowledge that pass all the argument of the earth,
And I know that the hand of God is the promise of my
own,
And I know that the spirit of God is the brother of my
own,
And that all the men ever born are also my brothers, and
the women my sisters and lovers,
And that a kelson of the creation is love,
And limitless are leaves stiff or drooping in the field....

_____ Walt Whitman

Our Memory of Ryan

Ryan, our beautiful brown eyed boy
Whose laughter tickled hearts with joy
Mischievous innocence tested waters of life
Gentle tears betrayed emotions of turmoil and strife
Transformers, braces, swim clubs and planes
Led your dreams, and growth through teens
Fast cars, fast life zoomed as years into minutes
You journeyed earth quickly filling life's folder.
Young man, actor, son and brother
Intimate roles impacting one another
The stage was set, but with regret
Glam, money, fame drew you away
Dad, mom, sister, traditions astray
The sun rises and sets in rhythm of days, months and years
As we witness time's progression,
Cups brim of sorrow and tears and many laughs, hugs and
cheers
Once it was said we are but players in a great play
That goes on to live another life, another day.
You were a candle in the wind burning quick and bright
Eyes turned heavenward see your light
Your presence within us lingers in memory of warmth and
love.
Carrying your spirit in a torch of light within our dancing
hearts

Your loving family

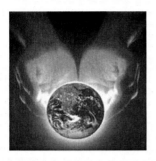

Challenges become easier when one accepts that life is created by our choices from beginning to end. Our journey through the labyrinth of life is all about the process; how we improve through degrees of challenges presented to us. Daily life propels us through constant evolving change. Change can be as a breath of spring air, teaching us to appreciate pleasure and greatness of all that is living. Love feels abundant as creative forces manifest ideas into reality and we say "Life is good." Change can be as a beautiful sunset calming our spirit into acceptance that everything arises and sets. Endeavors mirrored in the mind as a still pond brings peace and we say it will be what it will be. Change can be as a frozen lake, hardened to with stand fears of unknown realms, grief and loss.

Each of us are consciously or unconsciously writing stories of our lives, and knowing this is but one chapter of a larger book elicits inner peace.

We are given a gift of many lifetimes to reach spiritual enlightenment, sharing the universal goal within our soul to return to our origins.

There is only breath that carries us from the first cry at birth to the last sigh at death. However you fill each breath is your choice but remember we are interconnected beings from a source of great intelligence and immense love inspired by a grand purpose of creation for the greater good for all.

Thank you to my many guides in life in this world and beyond.
We are seekers of credibility, truth and knowledge. Years of college in health sciences assisted my direction in life and outer personality but greater education comes from living fearlessly, loving intensely, and living in gratitude for each new day. It is not the degree or diploma, nor the home or car, nor the clothes or money that defines who we are. They are temporary props of the illusion created by our ego. **Life itself is the true miracle.**

Perhaps there is a reason you were guided to read the book.
Maybe ideas needed clarity, a question an answer or a feeling awakened.
Addictions wound lives and leave many to feel isolated and alone. If you know of someone who may unlock an emotional door and seek help by reading the story then please recommend the book. It may plant seeds that one day grow in the light of love.
The more we can inspire an awakening for reconnecting to our universal source the sooner we can all fulfill our grand purpose.

Please tell others about the book, in this manner messages will spread and those relearning to channel will join the worldwide challenge to bring a healing light into our world for a "New Dawning Age of Peace" foretold to reign for a thousand years.

Linda has practiced energy healing for 30 years as a Bioenergetics Therapist, Reiki Master and herbalist and continues to practice at **Aspen Grove Spa for Wellness** in Calgary Alberta
www.aspengrovespa.net

May you find solace within, a joyful heart, and healing for self, loved ones and the only world we have.

Blessings to All